MARRIED TO A
PSYCHIATRIST

A MEMOIR

DAN PROCHODA

MARRIED TO A PSYCHIATRIST, LLC

Library of Congress Control Number: 2023921916

Published by: Married to a Psychiatrist, LLC

Woodland Park, Colorado, USA

Visit our web site at www.MarriedToAPsychiatrist.com

WARNING

This book contains profanity, describes a couple of sexual acts, and explores themes around biased thinking, homophobia, disparaging behaviors, dysfunctional family dynamics, and other topics that sensitive readers may find offensive or disturbing. Think of it like an R rated movie.

Reader discretion is advised.

DISCLAIMER

This book is not intended to be used to treat any medical or psychiatric conditions, which is an odd thing for me to say since this book doesn't attempt to treat any medical or psychiatric conditions.

Additionally, the views and opinions expressed herein are solely my own and do not express the views of the US Government, for whom I work, which is also an odd thing for me to say, since it's kind of obvious, but they asked me to say it anyway.

Finally, the stories in this book are true and accurate to the best of my ability to recall them, with a few exceptions:

- To protect the identity of those I talk about, I have altered or avoided using their names entirely. I humbly request that those of you who know their identity do the same.
- My best friend's accent does not make women purr; I totally made that up.
- Please consider anything in quotes as nothing more than an earnest attempt to recreate one or more conversations I've had in the past.

- Hmmm... what was that last thing... oh yeah! According to the American Psychiatric Association, my wife isn't a psychiatrist.

I should probably explain that last one...

While an engineer might be defined as one who engineers, and a teacher might be defined as one who teaches, a psychiatrist is not defined as one who performs psychiatry. This is because the American Psychiatric Association (APA) specifies that a psychiatrist must either be a Medical Doctor (MD) or a Doctor of Osteopathic Medicine (DO). My wife is a Doctor of Nursing Practice (DNP). As opposed to a Doctor of Philosophy (Ph.D.), which is a research-based degree, the DNP is a clinical doctorate, just like the MD and DO.

Additionally, my wife has earned dual master's degrees as both a family nurse practitioner (FNP) and a psychiatric nurse practitioner (PMHNP). Having practiced psychiatry in Colorado, Arizona, and Washington, her degrees grant her the ability to practice psychiatry independently and under her own license and prescriptive authority. (Note: regulations concerning independent practice for NPs vary by state).

Having spent over 15 years performing all the same duties as a psychiatrist (to include serving as medical director providing oversight to MDs, DOs, and PMHNPs), while seeing all the same patients, using the same diagnostic standards, and prescribing all the same medications and treatments, I think she's earned the right to be called a psychiatrist, even if the APA disagrees.

Besides, why would I call a doctor who practices psychiatry anything but a psychiatrist? That would just be... silly.

To Fredi (my wife):
I love you.

OK, enough with the mushy stuff; let's get on with this story.

CONTENTS

PART I
THE PSYCHIATRIST AND ME

1. Asleep   3
2. The Psychiatrist   10

PART II
THE INSIGHTS

3. I Judged You At "Hello"   17
4. Turning Into The Storm   29
5. The Apple That Didn't Fall Far From The Christmas Tree   41
6. The Perfect Woman   48
7. A Car Named Happiness   60
8. Don't Shit On Me   69
9. High School Swat   77
10. You Made Me Angry   83
11. The Boundary   90
12. Burnt Hashbrowns   96
13. The Many Faces Of Fear   101
14. Me Big Man, Me Wear Big Condom   110
15. Men Are Pussies   118

PART III
A CLOSER LOOK

16. Judgment Day   133
17. The Saint   139
18. Death Of A Saint   152
19. In A World Of Morons, Assholes, And Me   161
20. Shitstorms Caused By Should   166

PART IV
THE LEARNING NEVER ENDS

21. Ma, I'm Not Gay   173
22. A Healthy Kind Of Selfish   183

23. The Job That Wasn't Meant To Be   189
24. The Message   199
25. Happy Isn't Hard   203

PART V
STUFF YOU FIND AT THE END OF A BOOK

Afterword   209
Acknowledgments   215

MARRIED TO A PSYCHIATRIST

PART I

THE PSYCHIATRIST AND ME

1

ASLEEP

I woke up, and everyone was staring at me. Silent and expressionless, they looked like weary passengers observing a stranger who had fallen asleep on a train. Not that I found this odd, as I had indeed fallen asleep on a train, but why had their collective gaze fallen on me? Why weren't some of them looking out the window, reading a book, or quietly talking amongst themselves?

Perhaps they thought I was homeless? A plausible conclusion, after all, I hadn't bathed since leaving the States and had been living and sleeping in the same clothes for a week. I'd also developed a nasty habit of dozing off during the day, a result of going to bed late, often drunk, and the cross-border passport checks that awakened me late at night.

My best friend and I had contemplated this trip to Europe throughout high school. We didn't think we could afford the journey until we discovered the Eurail Pass. Available to students for only a few hundred dollars, the ticket would grant us unlimited travel by train. We concluded that if we spent our days touring historically rich cities, and slept on trains at night, that the pass would cover the cost of both our lodging and travel.

Furthermore, by choosing a route that repeatedly crisscrossed Europe, we could maximize our travel distance thus providing us ample time for sleep. The plan meant sacrificing beds, pillows, and warm showers, but we didn't care; such hardships would be exploited later when recounting our tales of wild adventure.

A key topic in planning our trip was whether to bring our girlfriends. This was a matter of great importance to me, as being a pale, lanky, and socially awkward kid, I wasn't the type to find an overnight love interest in a nightclub or cafe. If I wanted a woman to sleep with, I'd have to bring her along. This wasn't a burden shared by my best friend. Besides being handsome, charming, and perpetually doused in masculine-scented perfumes, he spoke with an Italian accent that compelled women to purr. Fortunately for me, having recently found his one and only true love, of which there'd been a number over the years, he agreed we should bring them along.

Both my girlfriend and I were thrilled; her parents were not. Declaring their intent to keep their daughter safe, they prohibited her from going. I knew their concern was not that she'd fall from the back of a Moped or trip down the stairs of the Colosseum, but that she'd be spending her nights with me. Presuming their daughter was still a virgin, I held little hope of changing their minds. Besides, one can't argue with safety, and her parents knew that.

Realizing I would now be traveling alone, I suggested that my friend abandon his girlfriend as well. I reminded him that this was our trip, the one we'd planned for years, and that I should have never requested we bring the ladies along. I described how the two of us shared the same wavelength of thought, often predicting each other's next words, and urged him to consider how our interactions would make her feel.

Without giving him time to respond, I answered, "She'll feel unwanted and left out, like a stray dog following behind two men whose conversation she can't understand."

Pausing, just long enough for him to comprehend the depth of her loneliness, I lowered my brow in confusion before asking, "How could you do that to her... to the woman you love?"

Of course, he brought her along, and in so doing altered the nature of our much-anticipated trip. This would no longer be the adventure of two high school best friends, but the adventure of two high school sweethearts. The title of *stray dog* had just been transferred to me.

This fact was confirmed when our journey was unexpectedly cut short at a train station in the heart of Vienna. Having just arrived from France, I was orienting myself to the city map when he approached from behind and asked to speak a word. His voice was deep, a tone he reserved for only the most serious conversations, and as I turned, I noticed his girlfriend was watching from across the crowded terminal. I knew whatever he said next, wasn't going to be good.

Placing his hand on my shoulder, he took a deep breath and explained that due to unforeseen circumstances, he could no longer continue forth on our journey. I searched his eyes for justification. Had there been a fire? The death of an aunt? It wasn't his father's heart again, was it? With his hand still resting on my shoulder, he explained that his girlfriend was having her period. It was a bad one, very messy, blood everywhere.

I looked at him in disbelief, "Are you fucking kidding me? We've been planning this trip for years!"

He didn't respond but instead continued to explain that he needed to be there, with her, for her, to support her during this difficult time.

"Difficult time? It's a period! She has one every month! Don't you think she can handle it on her own!"

Again, no response, just an apology. Then, as quickly as we

arrived, he bade me farewell as they boarded a train to Milan. They intended to stay at his parent's house until she recovered from her condition.

Left standing on the train platform, angry and alone, I contemplated my next move. Rather than unleashing my anger on a wayward pigeon, I boarded a train to Stuttgart. I decided to visit my grandmother. I didn't know very much German, and she didn't know very much English, but that didn't matter; she communicated with smiles, hugs, and various forms of chocolaty indulgence. Hers was the universal language of love spoken by grandmothers worldwide, and I was eager to hear what she had to say.

The train to Stuttgart was full, but I eventually found a spot in which to wedge myself. Each compartment was designed for groups of eight passengers with four sitting across from four others. I didn't care for this arrangement since every time I looked up I was met with the disapproving scowl of the elderly woman who sat across from me. The two of us were almost touching knees, which made avoiding eye contact with her practically impossible. However, with no other seating options available, I settled in and resigned myself to her glaring judgment.

As the train pulled out of the station, I closed my eyes and became drowsy. The hypnotic clickety-clack of the wheels and the gentle rocking of the passenger car soothed my agitated soul. The only opposition to my slumber was the vertical seat back and the padded headrest that urged me to slouch, but my exhaustion, combined with the warmth of the passengers beside me, outweighed my discomfort and before long I was fast asleep.

When I awoke, I had that foggy and euphoric sensation one experiences after emerging from a deep and peaceful slumber. I believe this is the body's way of saying *thank you, thank you for giving me that, I really needed it*. I took a big breath of the musty air, tainted by the odor of a thousand previous travelers, and slowly opened my eyes.

It was at this moment that I discovered everyone staring at me; but why? If they didn't think I was homeless, had I been snoring? Had I said something in my sleep? I turned to look out the window and recognized the rolling hills that signaled our approach to Stuttgart. *We must be close*, I thought, *which meant I must have been sleeping for hours.* As I continued to awaken, I noted a chill in my upper chest and body, a feeling much different than the cozy warmth I'd experienced earlier. I surmised the temperature in Germany must be cooler and made a mental note to dig my sweater out of my backpack once we arrived.

Still in the process of waking, I reached up to wipe the corner of my mouth, and as my fingers slid across my chin, I immediately recognized the slick substance they encountered. Looking down at the saliva covering my fingertips, I discovered the source of my chill. From my collar to my crotch, from one armpit to the other, the front of my shirt was drenched in enough drool to fill a beer stein. The excessive volume of liquid indicated to me that my salivary glands must have been pumping since the moment we departed Vienna.

Time began to stretch as my mind kicked into overdrive. Had these passengers been watching me this entire time? I stared at the floor. I imagined the viscous strands of saliva that had been hanging from my lower lip and how they must have swayed in unison to the trains' rocking motion. I visualized how each string took its turn stretching and thinning before snapping into freefall. I considered how my audience had been exchanging glances and smiles while elbowing all the others, directing their attention to the slobbering kid from America.

I wanted to disappear, but there was nowhere to go, so I just sat there and waited for the train to arrive.

The awareness and mental connections that are made in the human brain during an event like this are astounding. Moments earlier, I was oblivious to the truth. I was enjoying my post-nap fog, wondering what my spectators found so interesting, feeling the odd chill in my body, and experiencing a host of other sensations one gets when riding aboard a train.

These were all disjointed thoughts with no association between them. But in that split-second I touched my chin, the pieces of the puzzle slammed into place: The saliva on my fingertips, the lack of sleep, the rocking train, the staring passengers, the straight-backed seat, the over-padded headrest that pushed my head forward, and the evaporative cooling that caused the chill in my chest. It all pointed to the fact I had drooled. Even facts I disregarded earlier made a second appearance, like the musty odor I attributed to past travelers, which I now realized was the stench of digestion wafting off my chest.

These facts had been floating around my head, randomly bumping around, until the secretion on my chin gave them a shared context. That was the missing link that caused all these disjointed thoughts to coalesce into a single horrifying realization.

To me, this is one of the most interesting things about awareness. How facts that seem unrelated can rapidly become associated provided the necessary connections are made. And that is what this book is all about, awareness. Awareness of how I was asleep in my life, much like I was asleep on the train. I slept through a decade's worth of time. I slept through my first marriage and an entire career. I dreamt I was successful and doing everything right, while failing to comprehend, I'd been drooling and doing everything wrong, that is...until I met my second wife, the psychiatrist.

Much of what I talk about in this book is embarrassing, immoral, and in a variety of ways leaves me wide open for judgment. I spent the better part of my life keeping these stories secret, ashamed to admit them, fearing the judgment they might bring. I've since learned I can't control the thoughts of others, no matter how hard I try. People can and will find a reason to judge me, whether it is something I control or not. This realization, and the ability to free myself from the need to mitigate their judgment, is just one aspect of my awakening that has benefited me profoundly.

But before I present the messy details of my life, I'd first like to introduce you to the little lady who made this transformation possible.

2

THE PSYCHIATRIST

I met my wife on a dating website. It was the picture of her straddling a full-size Harley Davidson in black leather that first caught my attention. *A petite, spikey-haired, bleached blond woman riding a motorcycle like that would have to have a fair amount of courage and adventure,* I thought. I wanted to know more.

Her dating profile was curiously unlike the others, which often read as if they'd been copied and pasted from one another. There was no talk of sipping wine before a warm fire, dancing barefoot on a sandy beach at sunset, nor anything else requiring the services of a *man who knows how to make a lady laugh.* Instead, hers spoke of training squirrels, associations with Tinkerbell, and the thrill of taking Sully and Petey out for a ride in the mountains. I recognized Sully as her motorcycle from the caption on her picture and concluded that Petey was the stuffed emperor penguin she had strapped to the backrest.

This woman had no bounds. She claimed the ability to wrangle any power tool built by man, expressed a desire to rule the world, and voiced her refusal to date any guy who still lived with his mom. How could I not go on a date with a woman like this? She was quirky, odd, looked great dressed in leather, and obviously could handle a motorcycle more than twice her size.

I decided to write her a message. I wrote that, although I enjoyed her profile, I was concerned by what I perceived as an apparent wild side. Therefore, before asking her on a date, I wanted to inquire whether she spontaneously danced on table-tops, as this could potentially lead to my embarrassment at formal dinner parties.

I laughed as I wrote that last part. I imagined a dining hall filled with guests seated at a table built for a queen. Near one end sits this little lady, restlessly squirming in her chair while tugging at the bodice of her overly constricted gown. Sitting across from her, her new boyfriend periodically breaks conversation with others to cast his stern-faced glances upon her. Desperately wanting to dance, yet feeling the weight of his disapproval, she becomes increasingly fidgety with the passing of each course of the meal. Then, no longer able to contain herself, she surrenders all hope of a lasting relationship and stands on the seat of her chair. Taking one small step up to the table, she pauses to acknowledge her guests with the slightest of bows, and then, with a mischievous grin, erupts into an Irish folk dance with such vigor and fury that her pumping legs send dishes flying, guests scrambling, and leaves her humiliated boyfriend splayed out on the floor, covered in gravy, while mumbling something about wishing he'd never asked her out.

The imagery left me in stitches. In just two sentences, I had crafted one of the most brilliant introductions ever made by man. Who else but me could have written such an imaginative, creative, and charming masterpiece? Pleased with my work, I reread my message, and while still chuckling, I hit send.

As is often the case, I regretted writing the message the moment I sent it. What the hell was I thinking? I knew better than to introduce myself to this woman with an attempt at humor. I could already see her perplexed face as she read my email. She'd think I was serious. She'd think I was an idiot. She'd think I was actually concerned she'd be so crude as to dance on a table at a formal dining event.

How could I have screwed this up? Three months of searching for just the right woman only to fuck it up with a childish-sounding email. My god, was it even possible to have made more of an ass of myself?

The next day, a message popped up in my inbox. She'd responded. I expected her to suggest I drown myself, or perhaps take some time to grow up before attempting to converse with adult women again, but she did none of that. Instead, she told me that she had indeed done a spontaneous table dance, and this is how I met Fredi, the woman who would eventually become my second wife.

Little did I know that this woman would begin a process of waking me up that would span a decade and continues to this day. She would help me see connections between different aspects of my life that I had been blind to, often because they were indiscernible through the lenses of my own beliefs and philosophies. These revelations would not only change my life but would lead me to re-evaluate everything I knew to be true about myself and the man I'd become. It is a process that feels much like giving yourself a lobotomy with a fork.

But how could such a dramatic change happen? I mean, I wasn't a teenager, I was 40 years old. I had life experience. I was a decorated cop with an excellent service record. I was one of those *get-it-done* kinds of guys who *got it done* before anyone asked. I initiated and drove the development of several crime prevention programs, helped shape department training as an instructor in multiple disciplines, and excelled in every assignment I'd been given. Hell, I'd even been chosen as SWAT team leader! I wasn't the type of guy to stumble my way through life; I was a winner. I lived in a nice house, drove an awesome car, and saved enough money to go on vacation whenever I wanted. So, how on earth could she have turned my life around, most notably, in a positive direction?

Fredi would later describe it like this. *Intelligent people are often the hardest ones to treat. Their brilliant minds create intricate defense mechanisms that serve to rationalize their dysfunctional thoughts and behaviors. This is why some of the most successful and educated people, who appear to have everything one could want or need, end up leading unhappy and unfulfilled lives.*

I liked the way she phrased that, intelligent people, clever minds, intricate defense mechanisms. She's describing a special dysfunction exclusively reserved for smart people, which means I must be smart... let's go with very smart.

However, as I reflect on the lessons I've learned, the issues I've confronted don't exactly resemble the construct of a genius. Instead, my dysfunctions look a bit like a child's sandcastle, and my defenses, like the three-inch moat built to protect it. This begs the question, if my dysfunctions were so simplistic and poorly defended, then why hadn't I noticed them before? It's not an easy question to answer, which is why I wrote this book.

Let me start by saying that up until now, I've painted myself as a relatively successful person, and I suppose in many ways that's true. I've accomplished a lot during my lifetime, and in general, have achieved almost everything I set out to do. I've always attributed my success to the following set of philosophies:

- Life is tough – you've got to fight for what you want
- The secret to success is never giving up
- You must stay strong and not let things bother you

I've championed these philosophies to my friends, my

family, and even had one inscribed on the back of my personal-ized police *baseball card* that our Chief requested we hand out to kids. I considered them winning principles, grounded in opti-mism, and designed to all but guarantee success and happiness. I was certain that as long as I kept fighting for what I wanted, everything would fall into place, at which point I could relax and enjoy the results of all my hard work.

Had you told me that my winning philosophies were instead a part of my intricate defense mechanisms, I would have laughed while reiterating my accomplishments to prove you wrong. For this is how certain I was that my approach to life was correct: to challenge my winning philosophies was simply... absurd. But you already know where this is going, so let's put aside my philosophies and start the tour of my sandcastle.

The first thing you need to know is that I get along with everyone. I'm not one of those guys who judges other people...

PART II

THE INSIGHTS

3

I JUDGED YOU AT "HELLO"

One of my father's favorite expressions when I was growing up was, "You're being ridiculous." When my mom got upset at him for being late to the dinner table, he would say "Eva, you're overreacting, you're being ridiculous!" He used the same expression on us. In his house, one had to learn to control one's emotions, especially for us boys; he wanted us to grow up strong and not show weakness.

At first glance, this may not seem like a big deal. If anything, I was lucky. If I cried, I was only called ridiculous. There are plenty of kids out there who were called much worse things than that and often warned that if they didn't stop, they'd *really* be given something to cry about. And let's not forget about those kids who weren't given a warning at all; they were just beaten.

While the punishment may seem different, the underlying message is the same: your behavior is wrong; you need to change it. Well, I didn't want to be ridiculous, so the next time I started feeling tears coming on, I figured out how to suppress them. And as I got better at it, I started to understand what my father had been trying to tell me, because now when I saw other kids crying for stupid reasons, I thought of them and their behavior as, well, ridiculous.

Then, I started attending school. I don't remember much about my first few years, only three memories come to mind.

The first was that I liked this girl in my kindergarten class; the two of us always played together. One day she stopped coming to school and I never saw her again. It wasn't until the following year that I learned she'd died of cancer. I remember feeling sad. I didn't know what cancer was, but I missed her and knew I'd never see her again.

Second, I remember looking for leprechauns during recess. They would hide among the branches of the large oak trees that shadowed our playground, and my friends and I wanted to catch one to collect his pot of gold. I'm pretty sure I saw one once, but I never did catch him.

The third thing I remember was going to Rexall's drug store with my mom and finding an Oscar the Grouch doll in the toy bin. Oscar had big round white eyes, large bushy eyebrows, and a body covered in vivid green fur. I hugged him against my face and asked my mom if I could take him home because I wanted to sleep with him at night. She saw my excitement; there was no way she could refuse.

As we stood in line at the cash register, I noticed a kid from school approach. No longer was I hugging Oscar, I was holding him by one leg.

"Look what I got," I said as I raised Oscar into view, "I'm giving it to my dog."

"Cooooool!" my classmate said, "He's gonna rip off his head!"

"Yeah!" I replied, "rip it clean off."

Even in first grade, I knew better than to get busted with Oscar; everyone knows that only babies sleep with stuffed animals.

As I continued through school, I learned other things as

well. If a couple of kids grabbed my mittens and played keep away, I'd just act like it was no big deal. I knew if I chased after them, they'd just pass the mittens back and forth over my head and make me look like an idiot. And God forbid if I cried, then I'd never hear the end of it. It was all part of the code, and each year the code became more defined. How I dressed, what I liked, who I hung around with, it all mattered – everything mattered.

By the time I got to high school, I knew if I acted a little too happy or listened to a group like *Wham*, I was at risk of being labeled a homo. I knew better than to report a student's misbehavior to a teacher as I didn't want to be labeled a snitch. I also knew of the various social groups and the implications of being associated with each one. Getting thrown into one of these groups was as simple as wearing pants that were a little too short at the ankles because those used to be called high waters, and they were the fastest way to find yourself labeled a loser.

To handle all this, I did my best to remain unclassified. I had no athletic ability, none whatsoever, so there was no use trying to pretend I was a jock. I did, however, get to know a few of the friendlier ones, and that helped boost my image a bit. I liked the '80s dance music at the time, so my mom, against all my protests, dragged me to my first high school dance. She just left me there and drove off. It turned out I knew a few kids, and before long I became a regular at all the school functions. That got me dancing with girls and acquainted with some social types, from which invitations to parties soon followed. Once there, I drank a lot of beer and smoked a couple of joints, which got me in with the stoners and metalheads as well.

I knew a few nerds but didn't want that to be widely known. I fell in with that group when my dad brought home an Apple computer during the era home-based computers were unheard of. I figured out how to program it and wrote some simple games, which immediately gave me status among nerds.

As for the losers, I just avoided them like everyone else.

Overall, my ploy to remain unclassified and get along with everyone worked well. I learned to relate to different personality types, which made me more compassionate and understanding. I had a few run-ins with bullies and occasionally did stupid things, but I could usually find a girl to dance with, and if I could do that, then I must have been doing something right.

Once I entered the workforce, I found this ability to get along with others helpful. I knew how to show respect to my supervisors, even if I didn't respect them, which helped me get ahead. I also got along with my coworkers, no matter how different their backgrounds, which confirmed I was a kind and accepting person. For example, while working as a maintenance mechanic in a hospital, I had a rapport with almost all the employees. One day, I'd be the only white guy at a custodial staff party, slamming dominos on the table while drinking E&J brandy, Eark and Jerk as we used to call it, and the next day I'd be joining my first wife, a nurse at the time, sipping fine wine and talking travel with the medical staff.

Years later, one of my cop buddies told me how much he envied the fact I could get along with everyone; he said it amazed him. That felt good to hear. I considered this ability, to get along with others, one of my finest attributes, which is why I always listed it at the top of my resume.

Throughout this time, I never thought to ask myself: if I can get along with everyone, then why don't I have more friends? I had acquaintances who occasionally invited me over to work-related gatherings, but other than my two best friends, rarely did anyone call. One would think a person who gets along famously with others would have a lot of friends. Isn't that the guy who has a schedule full of dinner invitations, poker games, and random requests to have a beer? One day, the realization hit me.

I was a chameleon.

I wasn't getting along with all these people, I was disappearing in front of them. I'd walk into a room, identify who was there, and edit myself to fit in. I became so good at changing my colors that I could appear just as comfortable in a congregation of priests as in a gang of bomb-building anarchists. I had been practicing this shit ever since kindergarten when I got caught holding Oscar the Grouch, and I did it all through high school by trying to fit in with all the different groups.

I saw a quote once on a restaurant chalkboard that read, *Tetris taught me that when you try to fit in, you'll disappear.* That was me. By trying so hard to fit in, I had been making myself generic. My odds of being noticed and remembered at a party were about the same as remembering a single brick while touring an ACME brick factory.

Was it a surprise I had no friends? I wasn't giving anyone a reason to remember me. I was hiding everything about me that was different, which meant nothing about me was unique. How could I expect someone to call me, if they couldn't remember talking to me?

I've learned from Fredi that such behaviors can often be traced to one's childhood, so I began to think about my parents. My mom was born in Germany, and as a young girl, her father and brother (her only sibling), were killed in World War II while fighting for Hitler's army. Although she was still a teenager when the war ended, I believe my mother assumed the guilt for the atrocities committed by Hitler and his high command. This guilt is likely what led my mother to become the champion of the underprivileged. She didn't accomplish this by raising flags and protesting in the streets, but in her own way, like eating with her "colored friend" in the back of a restaurant during segregation or while expressing her support of the "queer folk" during the Gay Pride/Liberation Movement of the 1960s. Her contributions might have been small and may not have extended much past the boundaries of our family, but her message was certainly heard by me.

My dad's voice on the other hand was mixed. Having been born as an only child in Czechoslovakia, his family moved to Poland during World War II. As the Russian troops invaded and approached their city, my dad and his mother, who had been waiting for his father to return from a work assignment, decided to board one of the last departing trains to leave their city. It would be another 15 years before my dad would discover what happened to his dad. His father arrived at their home five days later and had been captured by Russian soldiers. Because he had fought against the Russians as a member of the Ukrainian Army during World War I, his name had been blacklisted, so they imprisoned him in the Gulag. They eventually released him in his 70s; he was one of the few who had been lucky enough to have survived.

Meanwhile, my father and his mother made their way through several refugee camps before boarding a ship to America. While working on the assembly lines of the Detroit auto industry, my dad earned his degree in electrical engineering from the University of Michigan. From there, he climbed the corporate ladder and became an international marketing manager, providing him the ability to travel the world.

Fluent in 7 languages, my dad loved to travel, and always attempted to speak in the native tongue of the countries he visited. Our family was able to join him on several of these trips, and he expected his three boys to be respectful, try the local foods, and visit whatever cultural sights the region had to offer.

However, despite his overt love of foreign cultures, he was also a frequent user of ethnic slurs. And even though his go-to expression was to, "Do it the white man's way" (meaning to do it correctly), I'm not sure that you could call him a racist. His bias extended much wider than that, encompassing just about everyone except for himself. A day spent out with my dad sounded a bit like: "Look at that guy's nose; it's huge; it's a surprise he can even walk with that thing, and his wife sure could stand to lose a few pounds, maybe that's why she wears a bedsheet for a dress, and wait, what is that? Their car? What a piece of junk! Just look at it; the tires are about to fall off, and can you believe..."

He could go on like that for hours, so, when he threw in a racial slur, it was just another adjective that was quickly lost in the long stream of criticisms of anything, or anyone, that crossed our path.

The attitude of my parents shaped the environment I was raised in and influenced the man I became. In other words, I was raised to shake your hand, appreciate your heritage, gladly try your food, respect your viewpoint, vote for your rights, and throughout it all, judge the hell out of you. Invite me to dinner, and from the time I walk into the dining room until I sit down a few seconds later, I will have already classified everyone in the room including the cat hiding under the table. Before saying hello, I will have already decided who I will sit next to, and who I will ignore. I can do this so quickly because I have rules. Rules like, if you're fat, you're lazy. If you're a man and a bit too friendly, you're probably gay. If you wear a crucifix or live in the mid-west, you're a Jesus freak, and if you have a Southern accent or a disability, you're stupid. And whatever you do, don't mention metaphysics or nature-based medications, because that just tells me you are out of touch with reality.

So, why did I become a chameleon? Because while I was busy judging the hell out of you, I was sure you were doing the same thing to me. And since I was judging you for everything different than me, then the best way to keep you from judging me, was if I was just like you.

But why was I so afraid of being judged? Well, let me ask you this question. To which high school group does a kid belong who has no athletic ability, can't tell jokes, needed to be dragged to the high school dance by his mom, only had two friends, got picked on by bullies, and was never specifically invited to any parties, but only showed up because his best friend had been? That's right. I was avoiding the losers like the plague because I hoped like hell that you wouldn't label me as one.

I was forty years old, and it would appear nothing had changed since high school. I was still ranking people, I was still trying to hang out with the cool kids, and I was still hiding my true identity in a desperate attempt to keep anyone from labeling me a loser.

Now, realizations such as this are often life-changing, but not for me. I wish I could tell you I've somehow transformed into the kind of accepting person I've always claimed to be, but I haven't. I'm still judgmental as hell. But that's why Fredi gave me a tool, and it's one I leverage quite heavily. It's a question to ask myself when I think I know something about someone, when maybe I don't. The question is, "What story am I telling myself?"

I used this question several years ago when I moved to Tucson, Arizona. In an effort to make new friends, I joined a hiking group that had organized a twilight trek into Sabino Canyon, a popular park for tourists and locals visiting the Coronado National Forest. As we stood in the parking lot awaiting more hikers, I met a guy who was fit, well-dressed, and new to town. The two of us hit it off from the start. The night was calm, the temperature cool, and the full moon found the perfect spot to backlight the giant Saguaro cactuses that stood like soldiers atop the towering canyon walls. It was a magnificent hike, one filled with adventure, stunning views, great conversation, and the prospect of having met a new friend.

Afterward, the organizers of the hike invited us to join them for pizza. I was thrilled because the opportunity to chat with my new friend over a cold glass of cold beer appealed to me. Upon arrival, I parked my car and paused to remove my socks. We had crossed several flooded bridges during the hike and my feet were soaked. As I entered the restaurant a few minutes later, I saw my new friend seated at the center of a long table already surrounded by other hikers. He noticed me and gave me a small wave to let me know he hadn't chosen the seating arrangements. Disappointed, I smiled my understanding while giving a small wave back.

I scanned the group and located the last remaining chair at the far end of the table. Seated by this chair was an unkempt young woman, a bit too pudgy for my tastes, a tall gangly kid with red hair and thick glasses, and a dark-haired fellow who I can't seem to remember very well. As I looked at these three, it became clear why the others had chosen to sit elsewhere. I should have known better than to remove my socks; those who arrive late to gatherings are condemned to sit among the undesirable.

Not willing to ruin an otherwise fantastic evening, I turned to leave. As I began walking out the second set of doors, it occurred to me just how quickly I had judged these three. My assessment had been entirely visual in nature; I knew nothing about them. I paused, just long enough to consider Fredi's question, *what story am I telling myself,* and realized that my decision to leave was entirely based on a split-second assumption. I couldn't deny it, my verdict identifying these three as losers lacked evidence, so, I decided to take a chance. I pried open my judgmental mind, went back inside, and took my seat at the end of the table.

While I scanned the beer menu for something refreshing to drink, I overheard the gangly kid telling the others about his volunteer efforts to remove invasive Buffelgrass from the Sonoran Desert. Of all the topics that this young man could have mentioned, I could think of none better from which to learn my lesson. Removing invasive Buffelgrass from the Sonoran Desert was precisely the type of mind-numbing topic that I'd expect three losers from Tucson to be talking about. This young man had just confirmed in less than 5 seconds what I'd known all along; I should have gone home.

As I contemplated my exit strategy, I realized just how fast I had swapped out one judgment for the next. I was still telling myself stories. *Just listen*, I reminded myself, *listen and ask questions, but don't judge.*

This was a new approach for me. My habit had always been to judge. Sure, I might listen, smile, and even pretend to be interested by asking questions, but my attention was always drawn to the commentary in the back of my mind; the same commentary that had judged these three as losers. This night would be different. Perhaps for the first time in my life, I would not be listening to my thoughts, but instead, would be listening to what these three would tell me.

The redhead kid began by telling us how he and his group of volunteers use radios, maps, and spotters to locate buffelgrass deep in remote stretches of the surrounding desert. The rocky vistas, flowering cactuses, and dramatic sunsets lend the Sonoran Desert an undeniable beauty, yet, as all the locals know, it's a dangerous place to visit. Every year, thirsty hikers are killed by its dry, unyielding heat, while those who stride unaware face the ever-present risk of stumbling onto scorpions, rattlesnakes, and a variety of other venomous reptiles and prickly plants.

The volunteers who do this work carry shovels, pickaxes, and plenty of water to drink so they can toil for hours to scrape the invasive grass from rocky crags and crevices before killing the remaining seeds with their packed-in herbicides. They choose to do this work because the invasive buffelgrass, introduced in the 1930s by ranchers seeking to feed their cattle, crowds out native plants, alters the ecosystem, and increases the severity of wildfires that endanger the surrounding communities each year.

As I listened, I heard the passion in his voice. He treasured the desert for both its beauty and its danger. He valued the hard work for keeping him in shape and relished the challenging environment to hone his survival skills. What I found most noticeable was the pride he felt in working alongside the Forest Service Rangers who he held in such high regard. These Rangers and volunteers were his friends, his mentors, and the people he relied on to keep him safe. They were bound by a shared vision of a healthier desert and were committed to a task that brought meaning and joy to their lives.

I was familiar with the type of connection; I'd experienced it myself. He was describing the camaraderie and respect I felt for the guys on my SWAT team.

When he finished talking, I didn't ask his name, nor did I ask where I could volunteer; weeding the desert isn't my thing. However, I'm glad I stayed. While I didn't envision becoming friends, I enjoyed the conversation, and perhaps more importantly, had come to respect the man who sat before me.

As for Ms. Pudgy Bottoms, she was a bit shy and didn't talk much. The two of us bantered back and forth a couple of times and I found her funny, witty, and more than capable of injecting a solid dose of insight into our conversation. Interestingly, I found her more attractive as the evening progressed. It happened in little doses, like noticing the brightness of her eyes and the upward curl at both ends of her smile. This observation had nothing to do with the beer, I drank only one, but because I'd allowed myself to see more of her than just her pudgy bottom. Had I been looking for someone to date, I may have asked her for a number.

The most notable observation of the evening, however, was

dedicated to that third fellow, the one with the dark hair. For some reason, I can't recall what he liked, how he dressed, what he did, or even what he said. He was sitting directly across from me, so I know we talked, and due to his positioning, we must have made eye contact.

I've thought long and hard about this guy, and there's only one explanation that seems to explain my inability to recall him...

Chameleon.

4

TURNING INTO THE STORM

The pastor presiding over the funeral of Fredi's uncle didn't want to miss the opportunity to speak before such a large crowd, so he decided to use the occasion to share his latest sermon.

He spoke of life and compared ours to a journey aboard a wooden ship that voyages across the sea. Along our routes we would encounter various storms to contend with, troubled marriages, problems at work, unexpected catastrophes, and these storms would send waves that would batter our hulls and winds that would rip our sails. We must, however, persevere, he insisted, because a life well-lived sails headstrong into these storms, enduring the pounding waves and punishing winds, while refusing to surrender or abandon ship. For it is these distinguished vessels that become known as the unsinkable, the most cherished among the fleet, and therefore the most deserving of fanfare as they complete their voyage home to be welcomed into the Kingdom of Heaven.

I'd heard a similar sermon before, it goes, *life's a bitch, and then you die*. And in a sense, I suppose I believed that. In my mind, the people who thought life was easy were the ones who ended up homeless; they were the ones looking for handouts. If I wanted a good life, I'd have to make that happen. I'd have to work hard and put in those extra hours on the job. I'd have to do my time, earn my stripes, and move up the chain of command.

My thoughts on creating a life at home were much the same; it takes hard work and isn't easy. When I married my first wife, I knew I didn't love her, but I still put the ring on her finger. We had a great time together, and although I considered her to be one of my best friends, cupid never shot an arrow my way.

I'd been dating her for several years when both my friends and family began asking when I planned to get married. "You should marry her and have children," my parents said, "you can't wait too long. There's only a certain window in which a woman can bear children and after that, it's too late." My friends at work were echoing a similar message, "She's a good woman and the two of you look good together; you should marry her." The message then started playing in my head as well. *Yeah,* I told myself, *I can't wait too long, I should get married and have kids.*

The only problem was that I didn't want to marry her. I knew the clock was ticking, even faster now that everyone was talking about it, but I just couldn't do it. I had to find someone else. So, I broke up with her and spent the next year on a quest to find my true love, but ultimately, I failed. Meanwhile, she spent the year crossing the country as a traveling nurse before returning home. We met, talked, slept together, and before I knew it, I was inviting her to move back in. I tried my best, but time had run out; I needed to start my family.

On the night before my wedding, my best man asked whether I loved my fiancée. "No," I replied, "I don't, but what is love?" I then explained that love is a temporary feeling of passion caused by the hormones of youth, brought about by exploring intimacy with someone new, and in time, is destined to fade as the relationship matures. Therefore, I asserted, it is friendship and not love that is the key to a happy and enduring marriage, and since I considered my bride to be such a dear friend, I would simply skip love and jump directly into my everlasting relationship.

Feeling satisfied, I looked at the man who knew me better than anyone else and awaited his response. He looked me in the eyes, nodded thoughtfully, and then asked whether we should get something to eat.

Like clockwork, I got married, bought a house, had a son, and settled into middle-class suburban life. It didn't take long for the reality of my decision to catch up with me. I married this woman knowing I didn't love her, and now we were bound together *until death do us part*. However, I was committed, and knowing it was too late to back out, I played my role as promised. It was simple. All I had to do was follow the script. Get up, kiss the wife, take the kid to school, go to work, come home, watch TV, and go to bed. The next morning, I wake up and do it all over again.

It was repetitious, but I presumed that this was what married life was supposed to feel like. We were getting older now and had adult responsibilities; the pleasurable years were in the past. It made sense that life would be more predictable and boring; that's what maturity and adulthood are all about, right? And from the feedback I was getting, our relationship was a good one. People said we made a great couple and that we seemed to care a lot about each other.

I took pride in hearing these comments; I worked hard to be a good husband. I was supportive and loving and always made a point to tell her how good she looked. I gave her mushy cards with flowers and sat next to her because that's what a good husband does. We'd be sitting under the stars, and I would think to myself that on a night like this, a loving husband would put his arm around his wife, so that's what I would do. I even once criticized a neighbor for not being more touchy with his wife. "Don't you care about her?" I asked.

I used the same approach with the decisions we made and the things we did together. Most of the time we went to the restaurants she wanted to go to because a good husband doesn't mind sacrificing his dinner choice for his wife's. If she wanted to spend Christmas with her family instead of mine, we spent it with hers. I took pride in these decisions; I considered it a necessary part of being an honorable and chivalrous man. I told myself I didn't mind doing these things for her because it was what I should do, which therefore meant, it was the right thing to do.

But inside, I did mind, and sometimes I minded a lot, like when she made dinner plans without asking me first. I'd come home from work, and she'd tell me we were scheduled to eat at our neighbors' house.

"What? I planned on staying home tonight. I was going to relax."

"Well, it's too late," she'd say, "they're expecting us."

"Why don't you ask me first? You keep doing this to me. You never ask. Can't you just ask me first?"

Of course, we ended up going; I had to. The neighbors already prepared dinner. It wasn't like it was their fault she didn't ask.

At other times I'd make plans, but she'd want to change them to do something else. It wasn't often I stood by my decisions, but occasionally I would, and that's when she'd start to beg. I'd say no, but she'd keep begging. "Please can we see a movie tonight, pleeeeaaasssse?" She knew I'd break down. Whatever it was, if it was that important to her, how could I say no? In the beginning, I didn't let it bother me, but the longer we were together, the worse it became.

I didn't want to be married to her, but what could I do? It had been my choice. I chose it when I bought the ring, when I proposed, and when I walked down the aisle to say, "I do." And it wasn't like she gave me a reason for a divorce. Perhaps if she had thrown a vase at my head, or had given the boy who lived across the street a blowjob while he sat bare-bottomed on my pillow, then I might have had a reason, but she did none of that. If anything, she was a social, loving, and responsible wife. What could I say? "Your honor, I demand a divorce because, on said date and time, this woman sitting before you had the audacity to make dinner plans without asking me first?"

No, I'm afraid not. There was only one way out of this relationship, and that was death. So, that's where my mind went. Not as in planning it, but more like daydreaming about it. We'd be moving furniture into the basement, and I'd imagine her slipping and falling down the stairs, or we'd be shopping, and I'd see her stepping off the curb into the path of a passing bus. These images weren't bloody or gory, even when the bear dragged her out of the tent, they just contained enough detail to confirm that I'd been freed of my vows. That's why a knock at the door was all it took to conjure up a policeman waiting to inform me that, with regret, there'd been a terrible accident just down the road.

These were the storms the preacher was talking about. Turn your ship into the storm, keep sailing, and never give up. And that's what I did. The winds were battering my sails, but I kept my course and continued to press on. I had given her my word, and now it was up to me to keep it. That's what an honorable man does.

Meanwhile, another storm was brewing over my career. When I got out of high school, my parents sent me off to college. I already knew what my future looked like; I was meant to become a doctor. That's not what I wanted, I'd dreamed of being a cop since I was five, but my father would have never allowed it.

His three boys were all slated to become doctors or lawyers. By the start of my third year in college, I was failing most of my courses and was well on my way to becoming an alcoholic. That's when I decided to stand up to my father and choose the path I wanted. I cleaned up my act, applied for the police academy, and initiated a multi-year quest to become a police officer.

The market in the early '90s was saturated with police candidates, and it wasn't uncommon for over 100 applicants to show up for a single position in the small towns, and up to 500 or more in the big cities. I tested for all the agencies: local, state, out-of-state, and federal. Each testing process took months and included written tests, interviews, physical fitness assessments, psychological profiles, polygraph exams, drug screens, and finally the coveted meeting with the Chief. I did all kinds of research before testing. I read websites, local news accounts, and participated in numerous ride-alongs with officers. Overall, the effort seemed to help. Most of the time I made it into the top 10 percent of the group, and occasionally I got to shake hands with the Chief, but when all was said and done, I received well over 50 letters that began, *thank you for your interest, but we regret to inform you...*

Finally, a tiny agency out in the plains of Colorado gave me a shot. The town smelled of cow shit, I was making minimum wage, my apartment had green shag carpet and dark wood paneling reminiscent of the 1970's, and I was just about the happiest man on earth. Our Chief believed in community, honesty, and in treating people fairly. I respected that man and everything he stood for; I've never met his equal.

The town's main street was a portrait of the old west, an image that was enhanced by the old Prairie locomotive parked at the train depot that served to remind visitors that this had once been a stop on the old Santa Fe Trail. I worked the night shift, and from my perspective, the population was split roughly in half between hard-working ranchers who dressed like cowboys and drove pick-up trucks, and hard-working migrants who dressed like cowboys and drove pick-up trucks. Both of these groups loved to drink on the weekends, and it wasn't uncommon for two or three of us to show up at a bar fight with 20 or more combatants. We'd be racing back and forth across town with lights flashing and sirens blaring and I absolutely loved it!

As much fun as it was though, the big city was calling my name; I wanted to go where the *real* action was.

I gave my Chief two years and then landed a job near Denver where my pay quadrupled overnight. The department was growing rapidly and opportunities to work on varied assignments were plentiful. It took me about a week, however, to realize that this department had a different vibe. Not only was this an upper-class neighborhood with far less action, but the officers who trained me seemed critical of everything I did.

During my first couple of years, I was stuck with a particular Sergeant who appeared to enjoy fucking with people, not only the public, but his officers as well. The decisions he made seemed questionable at best, often bordering on illegal, and when I wrote in my reports that he was the one who dictated my actions, he'd remove all mention of his name before locking and submitting the reports. I attempted to convey my concerns to the higher command but was told that if I had a problem, I needed to settle it with him. It didn't make sense; no one wanted to work with this guy. That's why his shift was always filled with new officers like me who lacked the seniority to choose any other.

On more than one occasion I was told that the way to get ahead in the department was to act as an informant against the other officers. I was told that it's difficult for a supervisor to know what's going on, so informants help them manage their crew. One day, an officer asked me why I never carried a portable phone, which in those days was the size of a toaster oven. I told him I thought it was bullshit we had to carry them, not only because they were bulky, but because the batteries died after a single call and would take the rest of the shift to recharge. Within minutes, the Sergeant ordered me to the station to explain why I thought carrying a cell phone was "bullshit". The officer who elicited this information from me was quickly promoted to Sergeant and Commander not long after that.

A few years later, a co-worker told me one of the sergeant applicants had obtained the questions for the promotional exam from an agency utilizing the same testing consultant. "That's cheating," I said; that's all I said. Apparently, my comment was overheard, because the next day both my co-worker and I were called into the Commander's office where we were joined by a second Commander. Assuming they wanted to interview us about this officer's misconduct, I was caught off guard when they spent the next two hours lecturing us on how we were creating a hostile work environment by undermining the credibility of the other applicants. We were assured that the officer who obtained the questions was not cheating but instead had demonstrated resourcefulness and creativity in his preparation for the exam. A few days later, it came as no surprise that this had been the officer that they had selected for promotion.

I learned to keep my mouth shut. I had no intention of changing or compromising my values, my honor wouldn't allow it, but that didn't stop me from testing for sergeant. My hulls continued to get battered and my sails continued to rip, but I refused to give up.

Speaking of refusing to give up, occasionally our department trained with a special bullet that was essentially a miniature paintball. The little bastards hurt when they hit, and would often leave a welt, but they allowed us to train realistically. One day, our training department put together a no-win scenario in which several shooters approached, but no matter where or how many times you shot them, the suspects wouldn't fall. The officers who were called to participate in the training, in this case me, were unaware of this fact and were told to act as if we were responding to a report of a suspicious person.

Being one of the best shooters in the department, as well as a member of the SWAT team, I had a lot of confidence going into these scenarios. As the shooters approached, I took cover behind my car door and opened fire on the nearest one. I was pretty sure I hit him, but to my surprise, he kept walking. The suspects came from different directions, and due to their angles, I was forced to retreat into my patrol car. I continued firing, but to no avail; they continued to advance.

Thinking they might be wearing body armor, I transitioned to headshots, but still, they came. I moved tactically, I shot steadily, and I reloaded quickly. I continued my fight until they were right on top of me, at which point I exited my car to unleash a final attack on a lone shooter standing apart from the others; at least I'd get that son of a bitch.

The point of this story, and the point of the scenario, is that our department had always trained us to win. If you did the right thing, or even mostly the right thing, you were deemed successful and the scenario would end. However, we had never trained to be in a situation we couldn't win. In other words, we had never trained to run away.

I was fighting from inside my running patrol car, yet it never occurred to me to throw the car in reverse and get the hell out of there. But why would I? If I ran away, who would deal with the problem? But now that I had time to think about it, wasn't escape a better option than dead? I didn't want to admit it, but I'd made a serious tactical mistake. I'd failed to consider all my options.

Here's another option that I hadn't considered: why would you turn your ship into a storm as the Pastor suggested? Why wouldn't you circumnavigate it or go the opposite direction? How many captains who lay dead on the sea floor wish they had simply turned their ship around? Is it worth turning into a storm just so you can be hailed an unsinkable ship?

When I worked at my first agency, I was held in high regard. I respected my leadership and knew that my co-workers and supervisors supported me. I was happy throughout the time I was there but then moved to the big city agency and immediately things went downhill. It was clear from the start that the philosophy of the department was different from mine, and that my issues with leadership went clear to the top.

Knowing I was unhappy, why did I choose to stay there for 13 years? Was it because the pay was so good or because I loved being a part of the SWAT team? I'm not sure, but I suspect it had something to do with my never-give-up philosophy. I'd been fighting for my leaders to change their values and the way they ran their department. While believing I'd eventually prevail, I failed to acknowledge that I'd committed myself to a lost cause. I had no control over the department's values and philosophies, and it's not like they hadn't told me that they were unwilling to change them. They told me each time they promoted a sergeant I disagreed with. They told me when they stopped asking for input into promotions. They told me when they scolded me for reporting questionable practices. They told me every time that they made a rule that didn't make sense. They told me countless times but I was too stubborn to listen.

Meanwhile, the same thing was happening at home. I claimed to be staying with my first wife because of my commitment, and I did so because that's what an honorable man would do. But who the hell was I honoring? I wasn't honoring her; I was lying to her. I wasn't loving her; I was keeping her from finding a man who would. I wasn't growing together with her; I was avoiding her. I spent ten years with that woman and hardly remember a thing. It was like all those years disappeared overnight. I'd shut down the day we got married and had been sleeping and drooling on the train ever since.

Honoring her would have been telling her the truth. Sure, it might have hurt, but what's worse, a painful breakup or a lifetime of deceit? As it was, I ended up having an affair; could I have done more to dishonor her, I mean, other than fantasizing about her death?

When word spread of my affair, I expected to get pummeled by the masses. I expected a long line of people to tell me how disappointed and disgusted they were with me, but as it happened, only one person did that. What I didn't expect was the dozen or so people who came forth to tell me how unhappy they were in their marriages. One woman, who had been married for over thirty years, even called me brave for leaving my wife. "Brave?" I asked, "I had an affair and ran off with another woman and you call that brave? That wasn't brave, that was the most chicken-shit thing I'd ever done!"

Riding out the storm of my marriage hadn't been the answer; I should have retreated long before and saved us both a ton of pain. I should have thrown my ship into reverse and gotten the hell out of there; that's what an honorable man would have done.

Fredi occasionally tells me about patients who will describe their misery while proclaiming how they wish God or the universe would send them a message telling them what to do. She says that, when they ask this, what they are really asking for is outside confirmation to do what they already know they need to do. She informs them that their misery is their message. It's how the heavens notify us that something needs to change. At times we need to weather the storm, and at times we don't, but regardless of the decision, the heavens have already spoken.

Fredi also points out that the underlying issue is often one of perspective, which is why it's so important to collect different viewpoints. One day, I voiced my concern to her about whether I should have stayed with my ex-wife because I feared how our divorce had impacted our son. She reminded me that children learn how to do life by watching their parents. She then asked, "Would you rather teach your son how to ignore his pain and stay in a broken relationship, or how to search for and find a happy and healthy one instead?" When I look at it that way, I think she was right. He not only witnessed the challenge of his parents searching for and finding better fitting mates, but as a bonus ended up with two stepparents who both helped enrich his life.

I'd spent a large part of my life sailing into storms aboard an unsinkable ship. I became so accustomed to the pounding waves and sail-ripping winds that I no longer checked my ship for damage. And that's unfortunate because, had I done so, I would have discovered that there is no such thing as an unsinkable ship.

5

THE APPLE THAT DIDN'T FALL
FAR FROM THE CHRISTMAS TREE

"C'mon Dad, let's put up the Christmas tree." my son suggested.

"I don't feel like it. Let's do it another day."

"But Daa'aadd, I'll be at Mom's house next week, let's do it now!"

"Nah, not today."

He was maybe seven or eight at the time and knew I wouldn't budge, so he went down to the basement to find the tree himself. I could hear him moving boxes around for the next few minutes, which was then followed by the sound of cardboard sliding across the basement floor. The Christmas tree box was heavy and taller than he was, and I could hear him struggling as he wrangled it through the doorway at the bottom of the stairs in preparation for his ascent. I knew the box was too big for him to carry, so pushing it up the stairs was his only alternative. As he began his climb, I heard the box repeatedly slide and then stop. I suspected the front edge of the box was catching the next higher step, thereby forcing him to readjust and reposition before continuing.

Amused, I remained in my chair, impressed by my sons'

determination. From my experience, that box truly was a pain in the ass to get up those stairs. Once he reached the top landing, he figured out how to put the tree together, and with the help of a chair was able to decorate it himself.

For me, holidays were never that special. When I was a kid, my mother would prepare some cookies and treats, and then help us set up the tree while my dad stayed in his office to work. Home computers were non-existent at the time, so with pencil and paper, he'd chart the day's stock market activity to capture the highs, lows, and averages for the day. He did this because the stock market was his hobby and passion, and in my opinion, afforded him the perfect excuse to avoid his family. After all, it wasn't like he was making money with these investments.

His insistence on remaining in his room throughout the holiday season would anger my mom, to which he would respond that she was overreacting and being ridiculous. But to honor his duty as the man of the household, which during those days was the social norm, he would come out of his office to place the final decoration on the tree: the pointy star that sat on top. That being done, he promptly returned to his office and shut the door as my mother pleaded after him to spend a few more minutes with his family. We'd see him two more times before Christmas ended, first to go to church, and then to open the presents.

Merry Christmas!

I hated that about my father; it felt like he didn't care. Fast forward twenty years, and there I am sitting in my recliner watching my son put the tree up by himself while doing nothing to make that Christmas, or any other Christmas, special.

Why didn't I try to make my son's childhood look different than mine? Was I too lazy to make the effort? Did I not care about him?

Fredi once told me that for her, Christmas was a joyous time of year with wonderful decorations, delicious treats, and a houseful of friends and family. She enjoyed Christmas because, not only did she love having visitors, but their presence provided a temporary haven from her abusive father. While Christmas meant safety and security for her, for me, it was a reminder that on a day when families spend time together, ours didn't.

I don't know. Maybe I'm just broken...

During my first year away from home, I lived in a college dorm with a kid I didn't know, who came from a place I'd never been. He spoke with his parents once or twice a week on the phone, and just before hanging up, he always told his dad that he loved him. The words sounded weird to me; my dad and I never said such things. Unable to deny the envy I felt for my roommate's relationship with his dad, I decided that maybe I could forge a similar bond with mine. I mean, why not? Maybe there was a chance we could connect like that too. So, the next time my father called, I eagerly awaited the end of the conversation and then I said it.

"I love you, Dad."

I caught him off guard.

He paused.

I waited.

And then he replied, "I love you too."

It was awkward. It felt forced. It seemed fake. And that was the last time my father and I spoke of love.

As for my son and me, it doesn't look much different. I've told him I love him, but it still feels awkward. Am I damaged? Do I just need more practice? I'm not sure.

The point is that sometimes the things our parents do suck, and sometimes when we become parents, the things that we do suck. And often a lot of the sucky things that happened when we were kids weren't because our parents wanted to suck, but because they are just people. People like me. People with baggage. People with dysfunctions. I wish I could have made things better for my son, and I presume most people reading this are asking, "Then why didn't you?"

I don't know.

Unfortunately, my son is grown up and it's too late to go back and try again. All I can do now is say I'm sorry that it wasn't different. I'm sorry I didn't listen to his stories or pay attention when he was showing me something. I'm sorry I spanked him for fussing at the dinner table, realizing as he vomited all over himself that I had just spanked my son for being sick. I'm sorry for those times when I promised to play with him after finishing my homework, but lost track of time and never did. I'm sorry when I didn't believe him, or didn't trust him, or didn't hold him, or wasn't there for him. Most of all, I'm sorry that I didn't fight his mother harder so I could spend more time with him after our divorce.

I'm sorry.

I express a fair amount of anger at my father in this book, but it's not about him; it's about the stuff he did. I used to be mad at him that he didn't play sports with us when we were kids. We were raised in the country, far away from other children, so we had no one else to play with. At school, we'd pick teams on the playground, and I was always chosen last. It wasn't just that I couldn't catch or throw the ball, but on more than one occasion I ran in the wrong direction because I didn't know the rules. I felt like an idiot.

But I understand why our father didn't play with us; he grew up during the war. Sports for him was stealing coal from the German supply trains while dodging the American fighter planes bombing the depot. He spent his childhood in refugee camps, looking for food to feed himself and his mother. The only reason he wasn't sent to the coal mines, a job that often led to fatal black lung disease, was because he learned English by listening to the American soldiers. He became so good at speaking different languages that the guards used him as a translator. Can I blame him for not playing football with me? Does he even know how to throw a football? He is who he is, and he raised me as he did, and that's simply all that happened.

Then it became my turn to be the dad. Unfortunately for my son, I didn't raise him much different. I suppose at some point my son will figure out he's pissed off at me, and that's ok. Our society has all these rules telling us we should honor and respect our parents, and I think that's a bunch of crap.

As a cop, I witnessed a lot of parenting failures. I heard the screams of the baby who'd been left alone in the apartment. Her teenage prostitute mom had spiked her juice bottle with alcohol to induce sleep while she serviced her client in a motel room down the street. And then there was the time I was dispatched to an urgent call from a father who caught his 12-year-old son masturbating. Convinced his boy was destined to spend eternity in hell, he plead for me to warn his son of the dangers of touching his penis. Is it any wonder people have sexual dysfunctions? I'm guessing that when that kid grew up, he was terrified the cops would kick down his door every time he got a boner. I've seen a dad fake his death so his kids would appreciate him, and another who didn't fake it but instead shot and killed his wife in front of their children before turning the gun on himself.

I don't think these people necessarily meant to be bad parents or had bad intentions, they were just mired in their own shit and lacked the tools to effectively deal with life. The guy who staged his death broke down in tears when he was interviewed, sobbing, "Nobody teaches you how to be a parent." But that's the point, just because someone didn't teach him, doesn't mean he isn't responsible for learning. And if that means his children no longer respect him, then so be it.

Fredi's dad was verbally and physically abusive and didn't see anything wrong with that. The physical abuse didn't stop until Fredi confronted her mom and told her that if she didn't leave her father, then Fredi would take her younger siblings and move them somewhere else. While her mom did leave, thereby putting an end to the physical abuse, the verbal abuse never stopped. So, Fredi chose to terminate all contact with her dad.

Interestingly, she maintains that her father's abusive nature did not necessarily make him a bad person. She says society often likes to label people as either good or bad, but that's rarely the case. People are complex. Her dad was an intelligent man who was well-read and gifted in gardening. While she holds him responsible for the abuse he committed, she acknowledges that he was beaten far worse by his father than any beating he gave to them. And if you look at it from her father's perspective, he probably thought he used restraint in disciplining his children. He may have even thought he was rather lenient, and that his kids should be grateful for his restraint.

Parenting is a topic that comes up frequently with Fredi's patients. They'll often talk about their anxiety when their parents come to visit. The anxiety might spring from their parents' verbal abuse, their disrespect toward a spouse, or even their hyper-critical comments regarding the hardness of the guest bed or the cleanliness of the kitchen. She reminds her patients that parents should be treated like anyone else, and that respect must go both ways. Sometimes that means saying, "Mom, I'm tired of your complaints. If the bed is too hard, or the kitchen is too dirty, then you're welcome to sleep in a hotel."

Respecting one's parents doesn't mean letting them walk over you.

For me and my dad, I realized that nothing I would ever do would be good enough for him because he'd always be critical of my decisions. Given that knowledge, I don't discuss my plans with him, nor do I seek his advice. I'll listen to what he has to say, but his opinions and words hold no weight in my decisions. With that safeguard in place, I'm able to have a decent relationship with the man. I can appreciate his strengths while allowing him to be dysfunctional in his own way.

We don't have control over how we're raised, but all that changes when we grow up. My son has a daughter now and I suppose the ball is in his court. This is his chance to shine and maybe change some of those unhealthy family dynamics.

I sure hope he does a better job than I did.

6

THE PERFECT WOMAN

I used to date the perfect woman, but now she's gone. Not just her, but all the perfect women... they're all gone.

I mentioned in a previous chapter that I had an affair, but what may not be clear was the thought process behind having one. My intent during those years was not to have an affair but to keep my marriage intact. I knew my unhappiness was growing, but I was still trying to salvage the relationship by any means possible to include following the type of advice commonly found on bumper stickers. The one that comes to mind here is, *Count Your Blessings*. That's short for, I'm not happy with my life, but if I can find a couple of things I like about it and focus my attention on those, then maybe I'll convince myself that life is grand!

So, I'd use this adage to contemplate my relationship with my first wife. I'd think to myself, I'm married to a social and adventurous woman who makes a lot of money, and because of this, we have a lot of friends and live in a nice neighborhood. That makes me happy, right?

The problem was that every time I convinced myself that life was grand, my wife and I would go to a party, or end up at someone else's house for dinner, and that's when things would fall apart. I'd notice how nice their place was, or how charming and pretty the guy's wife was, and before long, I'd start fantasizing about living in his house, sleeping with his wife, and smoking those fine cigars I saw in his humidor. This would make me envious, so to cheer myself up, I'd try to find reasons why I had it better than this guy. *Well, by owning such a large house, he must have a large house payment, and therefore he probably can't afford to go on vacation. And why do they need such a large house anyway, it's much too big for just the two of them. And while his wife might be pretty, she's an office assistant; it's not like she makes boatloads of cash, besides, her tits are too small. Who wants a wife with small tits? Not me!*

And that sums up how I counted my blessings. Focus on what I had that was better, as determined by me, and if I couldn't do that, then tear down whatever the other person had. I became quite adept at it too. If he made more money, then he was an overpaid pompous ass. If he drove a nicer car, then he was a show-off. If he ate healthier, then he was a rabbit food-eating health junky.

This tactic confirmed that my life was as close to perfect as possible: any less would be shameful, and any more would be distasteful. This approach also helped me articulate why life didn't always go my way. For instance, if I got a promotion, it was well deserved, but if someone else got it, then they were sucking up to the boss; that, or the selection committee was comprised of a bunch of idiots. Occasionally, I'd make an exception and acknowledge someone else's superior skills or possessions, but that only happened if I liked or respected them.

The way I saw it, life was just a big competition; one in which you had to fight to get ahead. That's why the fighter in me refused to give up. I was counting my blessings, and while I was at it, I was out there gathering some better ones. And what better qualities in life than to be strong-willed and unemotional? Not only did I know how to fight, but I knew how to deal with failure. If things didn't go my way, I simply wouldn't let it bother me. I'd just say to myself, *I didn't get it this time, but I will next time*, and with that said, I'd climb back on my horse and prepare for the next battle. You win some and you lose some, the important part was to stay in the game. I knew if I played long enough, then eventually I'd hit the jackpot; that, or I'd die trying.

A couple questions I never thought to ask myself were how amazing my wife had to be, how many square feet my house had to measure, or how rich I had to become before I'd finally be happy. I don't think I could have answered those questions, I just knew I wasn't there yet. And that's why my never-give-up philosophy was so important; it was the driving force that kept me going. I just needed to hang in there until everything fell into place. And it's not like I doubted that it would, after all, several of my friends had already found happiness. For some, it seemed to happen really fast. I suspected they simply had lower standards. It wasn't like I was jealous of their happiness, I just thought, *hey, good for you, I'm glad you like your 10-year-old car and your average-looking wife*. Me, I wanted more; I had higher aspirations. And that's what separated the winners from the losers. Winners don't settle for less, winners win jackpots, which is exactly what happened when I had my affair.

My mistress was everything I'd ever wanted in a woman; she was perfect. Smart, sexy, feisty, and adventurous; I couldn't have conjured up a finer woman in my fantasies. So in love was I that no one could have torn me away. It was beyond seduction and passion; it was a fucking inferno! Within four months of our first kiss, we left our spouses and spent the next three years in bed. This was true love. It had to be. Nothing else could have felt this good.

Our affair burned hot, so very hot, and then... it burned out.

Having been raised by divorced parents herself, my mistress struggled with the notion that she'd condemned her children to the same fate she'd endured. Compounding this issue was her concern that I would never become the loving father she'd envisioned for her children. I couldn't argue; her presumption was correct. One day, her four-year-old son joined me on the couch to watch TV. Always happy, he turned his little face toward me, smiled his always handsome smile and proclaimed, "I love you, Dan!" I stared back at him, silent, unsure of how to respond. I didn't even tell my son I loved him; how could I say it to hers?

She'd been watching from the kitchen and had seen enough. She left me within the week.

Her departure wasn't a total surprise, we'd discussed her concerns in the past. Yet, the speed with which she'd returned me to the singles market was still a shock. Nevertheless, I'd come out of my failed marriage and my fiery fling with a clearer picture of the qualities and attributes I sought in a woman. Fit, focused, and clear-headed, I was ready to move on. Winners never quit. Within a week, I signed up for an online dating account, and three months later, I met Fredi.

Years later, Fredi disclosed that her first impression of me was not that of a fit, focused, and clear-headed man, but a depressed one instead. She stated that I hadn't been eating, was thin and pale, and was living in a cold and dark house with locked doors and shut window blinds. She attributed my state not to any psychological maladies, but to a man who hadn't moved on from his ex-girlfriend.

I didn't think I looked that bad, but admittedly, I may have begun dating a bit too soon. A subtle indicator of this would have revealed itself had one inspected the *desired attributes* in the search filters of my online dating profile. Based solely on the checkboxes I clicked, the female I was seeking would have had similar looks to my mistress, the same cheekiness, sense of humor, body type, religious preference, hobbies, political orientation, and if there had been a checkbox for it, I would have chosen the same first name. This shouldn't come as a surprise, after all, she'd been the perfect woman.

Fortunately for me, Fredi was able to look past my hang-ups and decided to give me a chance. Over that year, our relationship blossomed as we talked, laughed, dated, and moved in together. Not long after that, I left her.

I'd heard a rumor, second hand, that my mistress was single after having broken up with her latest boyfriend. Not ever wanting to have an affair again, I told Fredi our relationship was over, that I never loved her, and graciously offered my assistance to help her move out of my house.

Within days, I was back in bed with the perfect woman. However, over the next few weeks, I noticed something had changed. I still found her attractive, but she wasn't quite as perfect as she'd been before. I began to see little imperfections in her body that I hadn't noticed, and her aura, the one that all goddesses possess, had dimmed. As time went on, I found myself irritated with her. This was peculiar, as she'd always been flawless in the past. I noticed the tasty dishes she prepared weren't as phenomenal as I recalled, and something about her assorted cats and dog were annoying me. One thing I cherished was the giggle she made while crafting a witty email or pondering an amusing thought. I'd always found this little bubbling overflow of happiness endearing, but even that seemed different and not as charming as I remembered.

Something had changed, I was sure of it, but I still found myself drawn to her. Not drawn, as in by love, but drawn like iron to a magnet. There was a force, an attraction, a pull of some sort that existed deep within me at the primal level, and with each passing day, I became more aware of it. It was a sensation so odd that I decided to tell her about it while admitting I didn't understand its origin.

As the weeks passed, we continued to talk. These were honest conversations, and I appreciated her willingness to help me process this strange and unexplained phenomenon. Then, one night, I was jarred awake by a clear and sudden under-standing of what this magnetic feeling had been. And just like that, it disappeared.

That night, I realized that I'd been using my mistress as a battery; she'd been powering my self-esteem. From the first time we kissed, I felt like I was the luckiest man in the world. This woman seemed way out of my league. After confessing the affair to our spouses, we were free to be seen in public and decided to attend that year's police department holiday party. While mingling with the crowd, we found ourselves talking to a single man who was charming, handsome, rugged, and manly. I stood there staring at him, intimidated, convinced he would sweep her off her feet and take her away from me. Then, in the middle of our conversation, as if on cue, she wrapped her leg around mine and pulled herself tightly into my side. She was claiming me, not only in front of him, but in front of everyone at that party, and I felt like a fucking god! It wasn't just in my head either, I was getting feedback from others who told me how lucky I was. Even the SWAT guys joked I should wife swap with them, and I'm not so sure they were joking. She was mine, and because of it, I was King of the World!

Unfortunately, the king was mortal. My insecurities kicked in. I became clingy. We'd go out and I'd constantly be on guard for men more attractive and charismatic than me. Every time she laughed at some guy's joke, or even smiled and said hello, my fear and tension would rise along with my suspicions that she longed for these other men. But at home, I felt safe, relaxed, and in control. I could tell that I irritated her; she wanted to go out and do things, to have a life, but the harder she tried, the worse my fears became, and the more I resisted. It wasn't surprising she left me that first time; I'd been trying to keep her in a box.

This attractive force I felt was my insecurity wanting to be fed. I wanted to feel like a god again but that wasn't happening. I'd been blaming her for losing her powers, but it wasn't her that changed, it was me. Fredi had somehow given me the ability to generate my own self-esteem, so I no longer needed to get it from her. Oddly enough, I think my mistress felt the difference too, because when I left, I'm not so sure she wanted me to go.

This hadn't been the first time my insecurities had caused such problems. I met my first true love in my senior year of high school. I'd tried out for a play and was cast into a supporting role as a Roman general. She was the student stage manager and had charmed me from the instant we met. Happy, confident, short, and sassy, she was wonderful. One evening, after rehearsal, I gave her and another cast member a ride home. The other guy was the naturally funny sort and had been cast as a Roman citizen who provided comic relief; he was a hard guy not to like. As we stopped to let her out of my car, the other guy whispered to me that he wanted to kiss her. I couldn't breathe. I didn't stand a chance against this guy. Devastated, I responded, "Go for it."

He moved quickly and stopped her at the hood of my car. There, illuminated by my headlights, standing before me as if on a stage, I watched through my windshield as the two of them kissed goodnight. My heart sank. They looked great together. If only I could have been more charming... more funny... more like him. Afterward, she walked over to my door and motioned for me to roll down the window. When I did, she said goodnight, and then leaned in and gave me the most delightfully lovely kiss. Her intent was clear; she'd chosen me.

That summer was unforgettable: late-night swims in a secluded cove of a nearby and always moonlit lake, after-hours hide and seek in a local park among dancing fireflies, and always a long kiss goodnight while leaning against my car during those warm summer nights.

The relationship went quickly downhill after that. She spent the next semester in Spain in a student exchange program. While away, she wrote letters describing in vivid detail the boys she'd met. She was partying, dancing, and staying out late at night. It was killing me. I knew it was only a matter of time before she'd be seduced. What woman could resist the charms of a young Spaniard on his home turf: his accent, his flair, the stone-cobbled streets, those quaint markets with fresh bread and flowers? Europe was built for lovers, and she was there, without me.

The following year she started college and invited me to see her perform in a college talent show. It was her and another chick dancing to Billy Idol's *White Wedding* along with some guy I'd never met before. She wore fishnet stockings, a tight leather miniskirt that showed off everything, and throughout the routine, this guy had his hands all over her. "It's just an act," she told me, "You've nothing to worry about." I knew she was trying to comfort me, but her smile and moves were telling me another story.

She wrote me letters describing these parties and how she was getting drunk and wild. I knew I'd lose her; it was just a matter of time. She kept telling me I needed to trust her, but she didn't get it; it wasn't her I didn't trust, it was the guys. I knew they'd seduce her, but my warnings fell on deaf ears. No longer willing to wait until she dumped me, I decided to venture out as well. I broke up with her time and again to date whoever, but lucky for me, she always took me back, until that last time. I tried changing her mind, but it was too late; she'd had enough.

I screwed up. Throughout all those years, she'd never once broken up with me.

It had been over twenty years since I'd seen her and I'd kept all the letters she'd sent. There were hundreds of them, each handwritten, and several pages long. In essence, they contained a daily journal of our past. An aspiring artist, she adorned the pages with roses, hearts, and other symbols of affection as expressed by a teenage girl. Fredi found my box of letters in the basement a few years earlier and had asked me why I kept them. "Those are mine." I answered, "They're just memories. What's the big deal? It's not like I tell you what you can or can't keep!"

One night, not too long after leaving my mistress, I sat in bed and read every one of those letters. They weren't as I recalled. It was like they'd been rewritten and switched out. These were letters from a young woman in love; a woman who was trying her hardest to make a relationship work with an insecure boy who blocked her every move. I'd treated her like a jackass.

My recollections of her wild summer nights in Barcelona, each with a different male Spaniard vying for her love, had been extracted from a single sentence out of the dozens of letters she'd sent that summer. She stated she had gone with her girl-friend to a club one night and danced. That was it. There was no mention of hot Spanish studs pressing their loins against her naked thigh, no talk of late-night drinking binges, nothing. The rest of that letter and all the others were filled with various combinations of I miss you, I love you, and I wish you were here. Likewise, her wild fishnet-stocking strip tease in college didn't amount to all that much either. The letters she wrote surrounding my visit, as well as those describing the rest of her time in college, sounded like any other student who was hanging out with friends and having fun. My fears and jealousy had embellished her words far past anything she'd written or done.

As I read the letters in bed, I let the pages fall to the floor while making no effort to keep them in order. I knew I'd never read them again. My heart was finally letting her go, and the tears were there to prove it.

I began reflecting on the other women I'd dated over the years. I always thought of myself as a nice guy; one who treated women with respect. I prided myself on not being one of those male sharks whose sole interest was getting laid. Instead, I was the guy who stuck around to meet the parents, buy the pretty gifts, and celebrate the monthly anniversaries. But now I was beginning to see a darker side of myself, the one I'd never known. It was true I stayed, but only long enough to find the next better thing. I'd been using the women of my life like rungs on a ladder, clambering over their bodies to reach the top of the pedestal in pursuit of the perfect woman.

I wasn't a shark, I was worse. I was a fake. My charades lasted for years, complete with professed love, flowers, and promises of commitment. These weren't relationships; I wasn't even there. I'd go out to dinner with these women and scan the crowds for females who were slimmer, prettier, or who had bigger boobs. I was constantly on alert for potential upgrades: in my school, in the mall, and on TV.

These magical women of perfection dominated my thoughts. I was addicted to them, none more so than the perfect women of my past. I was hyper-focused on them for years after these relationships ended, reliving their memories whenever I heard a song they liked, drove past a park we visited, or while sleeping with other women.

Fredi's sister told me that it's easy to think of a relationship as having failed when it ends, but she prefers to think of them as learning opportunities instead. Rather than feeling upset toward her former lovers, she feels thankful for the time they shared and grateful for the opportunity to have known them. Oddly, she told me this as we were moving Fredi's belongings out of my house so that I could return to my mistress. Expecting her sister to despise me, she gave me a warm hug and wished me well instead.

I couldn't reconcile her words, nor the fact she held no animosity toward me. My prior relationships didn't end with gratefulness and thanks, they ended with good riddance, lackadaisical loss, or in the case of my two perfect women, a deep and mournful woe. In hindsight, I don't think I could have appreciated the other women I'd dated because I'd been too busy searching for batteries. I'd been too preoccupied with finding a goddess to illuminate my dark hallways and power up my self-esteem. These other women were more like dead batteries, frustrating for only casting a dim glow on my hallways, yet better than being alone in the dark.

It was my insecurity that had made these women seem so one-dimensional, either perfect or not, but as I mitigated those insecurities, I began to see these perfect women for who they were. Human. Perhaps still attractive and charming, but no longer perfect. And as those levels of perfection declined, the scale began to recalibrate, and with that change, I began to appreciate the memories of all the other women I'd dated over the years. I could see their smiles, hear their laughs, and remember the good times we shared. And as these memories flowed into my mind, I began to understand what Fredi's sister had told me, because I started to feel thankful for the time I shared with them and grateful for the opportunity to have known them.

Of all the dysfunctions I've confronted, the loss of the perfect woman was perhaps the hardest one to adapt to. Even though I knew their perfection was a product of my insecurity, these women had been such a large part of my life that, without them, my world felt empty for a while. It was like I'd been on a life-long quest for perfection, and now the object of my desire had vanished. I'd go to the mall, alert for the goddesses who'd shopped there before, and go home disappointed that none had enchanted me. I'd open my porno magazines to those well-creased pages marking my favorite ladies and end up frustrated that none could satisfy me. I felt like a world-class fisherman, visiting all of my favorite lakes and streams, only to discover that all the fish were gone.

It took some time for me to regain my bearings. However, no longer distracted by magical beings and fantasies, I began to gain clarity. And with that clarity, I realized just how much I missed Fredi. I missed our conversations. I missed cooking together with her. I missed the feel of her warm touch against my skin.

It took her six months to forgive me, and more to regain her trust, but eventually, she let me back in...

And or that, I will always be grateful.

7

A CAR NAMED HAPPINESS

W hat's it like being married to a psychiatrist?

Occasionally, I get asked this question, and for those who might be wondering, let me assure you that Fredi and I don't do daily therapy sessions, nor does she require me to keep a diary, and never has she asked me to take out my crayons and draw a picture of something that makes me sad. In fact, most psychiatrists don't normally do that sort of thing.

Psychiatrists are medical professionals who write prescriptions and order treatments that balance moods, calm nerves, and help to quell voices in the heads of those who express a desire to light children on fire (Not all children, of course, only those who sport yellow boots and use their red wagons to ferry demons out of hell.)

The professionals with the comfy chairs and a box of Kleenex positioned nearby are more often psychologists, therapists, and counselors. Their work more closely aligns with the topic of this book, which is why you see a comfy chair on the cover rather than a tipped-over pill container spilling out Xanax.

This may lead one to ask how my wife could then provide such meaningful insight if her specialty is more geared toward the clinical side of psychology. I believe she's been able to accomplish this task because she has spent so much time trying to understand herself. Having been raised on food stamps by an abusive father and under the watchful eye of a religious cult, Fredi will tell you she grew up "mired in dysfunction". However, not willing to allow her circumstances dictate her life, she committed herself to reading books and undergoing therapy to address the trauma and untangle the dysfunctional thought patterns that had been the norm.

Members of the therapeutic community often say a therapist can't take a client any deeper than they themselves are willing to go and few, I believe, have gone as deep as Fredi. I wish they'd make a television show about her because she's brilliant at saying exactly what her patients need to hear.

I'll confess, however, that my impression of her may be biased. I say that, not because she's my wife, or because her ass looks so good in leather, but because I'm no expert in the field of psychology. Unlike Fredi, I never sought to understand my dysfunctions, primarily because I didn't think I had any. I never sought therapy, or read books, nor did I ever share with friends those things that make me cry.

In my world, psychologists and psychiatrists existed for those who were either crazy or weak, neither of which described me. Besides, I spent forty years honing my life, which naturally made me the most qualified expert on me. And since I was the most qualified expert, then what could some psychologist possibly tell me about myself that I didn't already know? More importantly, why would I even agree to see one in the first place, after all, I already had life figured out!

I mention this only to illustrate that even if Fredi wanted to perform therapy on me, she wasn't going to get far. I wasn't receptive, nor did I respect her profession. However, Fredi already knew this about me and wasn't bothered by this fact. She also knew she loved me, knew we made a great pair, and knew our relationship would blossom if she could only shed some light on my dysfunctions. And so, knowing that I would never agree to therapy, she did the only thing she could do.

She manipulated me.

Aware that my brother and I would never reject a gift, because it's not polite to do so, she gave us both a gift: an all-expense-paid trip to Kansas City to attend a *Heart Connexion Breakthrough* workshop. She presented this gift as a card wrapped in a bow. I opened my gift to read the card, and as I did, I cringed. Not outwardly of course, as that too would be impolite. So, as I stood there smiling my cringing smile, I thought to myself that this was not a workshop for me, but for people who stand on street corners offering free hugs to strangers. This was not my clan. The thought of spending a weekend singing and dancing while holding hands with a bunch of hippies wearing white gowns and ribbon crowns made me seriously uncomfortable.

Unfortunately, Fredi spent hundreds of dollars on this gift, money she could no longer return, and seemed genuinely excited for us to go. My brother and I talked it over, specifically focusing on how we could get out of this mess, but failed to develop a plausible strategy. Reluctantly, we succumbed to the fact we had to go, otherwise, the guilt would have consumed us alive. On the bright side, we agreed that the 8-hour road trip to Kansas City would be fun. It would afford us a chance to talk, and that was something we hadn't done in a long time.

In preparation for the workshop, I packed my pepper spray, but I didn't need it. The workshop wasn't what I'd expected.

There was no kum-ba-yah or flowery headbands, no incense-filled rooms, not even a single bard strumming a lute in the midst of a bath-house orgy. There were just people. People and conversations. Conversations that were sometimes guided, sometimes open, but always honest and real.

I enjoyed it. I enjoyed it a lot. We both enjoyed it. So much so that Fredi didn't have to pay for the next two sessions; we took care of that ourselves. The workshops cracked us open, just like she knew they would. The stories I heard resonated with my own but were told from different perspectives. Hearing them helped me develop new insights into myself and other people as well. I started to see the similarities in what we all wanted, both men and women, both young and old, and was baffled that I hadn't noticed this before.

But of all the observations I made during those sessions, the one that was impossible to ignore, the one that kept surfacing over and over again, was that out of all the people who attended that workshop, I was the only one without a beating heart. My emotional EKG had apparently flatlined a long time ago because even a rock would have shown more emotion than me. This simple fact puzzled me, which is more than what Fredi could have hoped for. She knew I wasn't the type of person who was comfortable living with unanswered questions; I was the type who searched for answers.

Now that I was primed, the next phase of my education began, and this is how it looked. Fredi and I lived our lives. That was it. We did all the stuff that other couples do. We teased each other and got into hellacious arguments. We had lots of sex and figured out what positions worked best. She talked me into family gatherings I didn't want to go to, and I talked her into family gatherings she didn't want to go to. We moved, we argued about money, and we did naughty things in public places. We laughed, got drunk, got jealous, and argued about furniture. We killed cockroaches, far too many to count, and named our clanky furnace after a cantankerous dwarf named Gimbly. We celebrated each other's accomplishments, triggered each other, and argued about how to raise my son.

Her approach to my education was brilliant. As she's fond of saying, there's no way to learn how to do life without doing it. You can read all the books you want, but until you jump into a relationship and start experiencing all the friction that goes with it, the knowledge won't do you any good.

I'm beginning to understand that now. I couldn't see my dysfunctions because they were buried in my behaviors and responses to life. They were hidden in a manner so intimately connected to who I am that they seemed a part of me. Many of my dysfunctions moved through me like reflexes. They were triggered without thought, just like the judgments I made of those three hikers in Tucson. Others were found in the habits and responses I'd formed to deal with difficult situations, not realizing that I was constantly turning my ship into storms.

I'd say our relationship was much like any other except for one difference. Fredi knows dysfunction, including how it affects both a person and a relationship. And so, when she'd see, or hear, or feel that something I said or did was potentially dysfunctional, she'd bring it to my attention.

One day, while walking out of our house to go shopping, I asked whether we should take my car or her piece of crap car. The piece of crap I was referring to is her Smart car, which she affectionately named Happiness. She named her car Happiness because it makes people happy. They smile and wave whenever they see it, not only because it's a tiny cute car, but because it's a tiny, cute, and brightly colored tie-dyed car.

After I asked my question, she stopped fumbling in her purse for her house keys, looked up, and asked, "You know how much I love Happiness, so why do you feel compelled to call her a piece of crap?"

"Hmmm, I don't know." I mused, "Let me think about it."

When Fredi asks a question like this, she doesn't tell me what I'm thinking or accuse me of being dysfunctional, she leaves that for me to figure out. And the truth is, although she may have her suspicions, she doesn't always know why I do these things. So, instead of blasting me with an accusation, she'll simply ask a question, and that works. It works because the question gets me to stop and think while giving me a hint as to the nature of the underlying problem, and just so happens to be far more effective at getting my attention than had she used an air horn.

But questions aren't her only tool; she also uses books. Over the years, there's been a number we've read together, either because they related to something that happened between us, or because she'd read them before and wanted to share. Some of these books had titles that made me cringe, like *Facing Codependence* by Pia Mellody.

"*Facing Codependence*? What the hell do you want me to read that for? I'm not codependent!"

"Just try it, I think you might find it interesting."

So, we'd sit in bed, and take turns reading, and before long we'd be talking about codependence, what it looks like, how it affects both of us, where it lives in our families, and by the time we finished, I ended up learning the many ways in which I was codependent.

Then, a few weeks later, she asked, "How about we read *Boundaries,* by Henry Cloud and John Townsend?"

"Boundaries? What the hell do you want me to read that for? I don't have a problem with boundaries!"

And so, we'd read, and I'd learn, and on and on it went. Over time, I began to enjoy our reading sessions, just as much as I enjoyed her questions. They taught me things. And every time I experienced another ah-ha moment, it made me feel good. I felt like, *wow, now I understand why I've been doing that!* It was a relief to be able to explain a behavior that I didn't even know existed in the first place. And reading these books didn't just help me, they brought us closer together too by increasing the intimacy between us. They helped us understand each other's thoughts, triggers, fears, and all the other crap that I'd always kept to myself. This was all the same stuff that had been bothering me for years, yet when I understood where the feelings came from, the burden of carrying them was gone.

I also enjoyed these conversations because it wasn't only my life that was changing during this time, but hers as well. Fredi is awesome, but she's certainly not perfect. And although she's great at understanding the issues that plague both herself and others, she'll never stop learning. Dysfunctions are a tricky bunch. Not only do the two of us occasionally find new ones to contend with, but we are constantly on guard for the old ones that have a knack for sneaking back into our lives.

But I'm not here to discuss Fredi's issues, only mine, which brings me back to the topic of cars. Over the years, I've made fun of lots of them, and usually did so expecting to be flipped off or insulted in return. However, until Fredi, no one ever asked me why. Like so many of her questions, I had to think about it, and here's what I came up with.

I make fun of cars for a variety of reasons. I often do it to tease someone I know. For instance, I'll tease my brother, the doctor, who's so frugal that I doubt he's ever owned a car less than ten years old. I also like to tease my good friend who drives a monster truck because, well, who wouldn't? In the past, I've made fun of cars behind the owner's back, but learned I was doing that out of insecurity. Like when I made fun of crappy cars driven by poor people, and fancy cars driven by rich folks who I would accuse of showing off. It was a tactic I described earlier where I was making myself better than others by finding reasons to look down on those who either had more or less than me.

However, in the case of Happiness, my motivation was not to tease, nor to assert my superiority. The reason behind my comment was slightly more complex. I'll start by saying that, if I don't like something, or if it's broken, or if it's poorly made, or if it's irritating me, then it's a piece of crap. Piece of crap is my go-to expression for describing, oh, so many things. I think those three words just sit on my tongue waiting for me to open my mouth.

In the case of Happiness, the phrase came out because I was irritated. And when I'm irritated, I become passive-aggressive. For example, if a friend is supposed to meet me for lunch, but doesn't show up, I don't tell them that my feelings were hurt because that would make me sound like a pussy. So, instead, I'll say something like, "What the fuck? Where the hell were you? I felt like a dickhead sitting there by myself!" By saying it like that, I sound more macho.

In Fredi's case, I know she loves her Smart car, and I don't really hate it. For those of you who have never driven one, they are surprisingly roomy little cars with plenty of zip. But with no hood and no trunk, these cars have no crush zone, and as a former traffic accident investigator, I know that no crush zone increases the likelihood of serious injuries.

The truth is, I was worried about her. I worry about her every time she drives that car, but I couldn't say that, could I? Tough guys don't worry. So, instead, I called her car a piece of crap. I suppose my rationale was that if I showed her that I disliked her car then maybe she'd get rid of it.

It would take me a long time to figure out the strength of admitting I was sad, worried, or scared. I avoided these words because I believed that they belonged to the vocabulary of the vulnerable and weak. However, had I told her I was *worried,* she might have listened and heard my message. And if she heard it, then maybe she would have given my concerns a bit more consideration. At least, that's what I keep telling myself, because she knows I worry about her, but she still drives that damn car.

She absolutely loves it!

8

DON'T SHIT ON ME

"Would you like to donate your change to the Children's Hospital fund to help fight cancer?" My mind considered the cashier's request:

No! It's mine! My money! Mine!
But now what? It's not like the other customers aren't staring at me right now, judging me, waiting to see if I'll stiff seven-year-old Timmy who at this very moment is shitting blood into his hospital bed gown while clutching his piggy bank full of nickels collected for his life-saving operation.
And who is this cashier anyway; what is she, 12? And just look at the way she's glaring at me. She's acting like, "Really? It's only 33 cents and you can't give it up for some dying kid?"
This is such bullshit...

"Sure, I'd be glad to donate!"
And nothing about helping Timmy pay for his chemo-therapy felt good to me. The whole experience just left me angry.

Later that evening, I told Fredi about my trip to the grocery store.

"This donation crap pisses me off! Everywhere you go they ask for money, and they do it with a frickin' megaphone so that everyone can hear what they're asking. Whatever happened to the good old days when they just set out a jar next to the cash register and let you decide whether or not to donate?"

"Well, if you didn't want to give, then why did you?"

"What am I gonna say, no? That I can't afford 33 cents to help pay for some dying kid's operation? It's extortion! They shame you into giving!"

"The cashier didn't shame you, you shamed yourself. She just asked whether you wanted to donate your change. You could have said no, and that would have been the end of it."

It took me a while to get it, but Fredi was right. I had shamed myself. I did it using a little word that I'm pretty sure was forged in the depths of hell by Satan himself. That word is *should*, and the astute reader will have noticed that I've used the word judiciously throughout this book. To recall a few examples, I *should* be strong and *shouldn't* cry. That was my first *should*; it was taught to me by my dad. Others include, I *should* be happy, I *should* donate, I *should* go to college, I *should* be a doctor, I *should* get married, I *should* have children, I *should* do what my wife wants, and I *should* work hard to get promoted.

Oxford's dictionary defines *should* as *used to indicate obligation, duty, or correctness, typically when criticizing someone's actions.* And that's what makes this word so sinister, it presents itself as an obligation to do the right thing but buried inside of it is a criticism. It's a word that says, ignore your feelings, ignore what you want, because I know what's best for you.

When I was dating my first wife, my parents told me I *should* marry her because I needed to start thinking about having kids. They said I *shouldn't* wait too long because there was only so much time during which a woman can bear children. That's the first problem with *should*, it's often thrown at us by someone who has good intentions, and often by someone close to us. My parents didn't ask if I wanted to marry her, they just said I *should*.

The next problem with *should* is that I took it from my parents and made it my own. *Yeah*, I thought, *I should get married and start thinking about having children.* And just like that, I made it my duty and obligation to get married and have kids. Suddenly, I found myself in a rush; I *should* get married, but I didn't want to marry my girlfriend. So, I broke up with her and gave myself a year to find true love, and when that didn't happen, I married her. And that's perhaps the most insidious part of the word, it gives a person justification for not following their heart. I could now say I had done my duty and obligation; I got married and had kids. No one could criticize me any longer because I did exactly what I *should*.

Now as I look back, I realize there was no rush. There was no ticking clock. I knew I didn't want to marry her, but I did it anyway. I also had it in my head that I *shouldn't* get a divorce unless I had a valid reason. I didn't need a reason; the court didn't care. I just didn't because I feared that my friends and family would judge me to be a dishonorable man if I requested one. That's why I was able to fantasize about my wife's death so easily because if she died in an accident, then I wouldn't have been blamed for leaving her.

Another *should* I followed was trying to get promoted, because one *should* get ahead and work their way up the chain of command. Throughout my police career, I tried to get promoted but never got far. I attributed my failure to the fact that I didn't play the promotion game, but I'm not so sure that was the only reason.

I kind of suck as a supervisor. I'm absent-minded and tend to forget schedule changes, people's names, and who I've assigned to do what. I'm also an optimizer who continuously wants to improve things, which means I focus on details and constantly change processes in pursuit of finding a better way. Who wants to work for a micro-manager who loves changing how things should be done? Umm... nobody.

I've worked for some natural leaders, and my former SWAT team leader was one of them. I complained one time about a guy on our team who was always rushing through the door at unsafe speeds during training. Team movements need to be controlled, someone needs to cover your back, and if you move too fast you risk stretching out the team and getting someone shot. The team leader explained that this is why he always placed that guy in the back of the stack, so he couldn't go fast. He said that when a situation arises that requires us to move fast, like getting to the drugs before they're flushed down the toilet, then he'll put this guy up front. I respected that leader; he was good at thinking of the different ways that a person's strengths could be leveraged to his advantage.

On another occasion, we were testing for a new position and interviewed a guy who liked to clown around. I voted this guy down; I wanted whoever was covering my back to be damn serious about his responsibilities. Our leader told me he was choosing the clown because people like him are good for morale. He said they create camaraderie and help reduce stress in the team, and he was right. Our team was better off because of that guy.

I had the tactical skills and knowledge but lacked the people skills required to build a cohesive team. If anything, I caused more frustration than cohesion. I kept asking the team members how we could improve until one day, one of the members had a fit. He yelled, "Aren't we ever good enough? For fuck-sake Prochoda, can't you ever say, *good job*?"

We were good enough. In fact, I think we were the best team

in the region and had proven it in training, but I didn't want to miss the opportunity to be even better. I was proud of our team but had failed to see the frustration growing within it. I wasn't tuned into such things as a good team leader would.

When I first applied for the leader position, I asked a few members what they thought. One guy told me he didn't think I'd make such a good leader but saw me instead as the person who advised the team on tactics. That's the person who sits in the command post looking at maps and pictures while planning the team's next move. He was right; I was a natural for that. A couple of the team members told me I was always four steps ahead of everyone else, and although I agreed, I didn't like the idea. I wanted to be where the action was, and that wasn't sipping warm coffee in the command post next to the Chief.

I was named team leader, but I wasn't the best choice. And while I believe a person can improve their skills, I think the natural leaders walking among us will always do a better job.

A wise man once told me, "Don't *should* on me, and don't *should* on yourself". Now when I hear the word *should,* it rattles me a bit. I think to myself, *don't you criticize me and tell me what I should or shouldn't do, I'll do what's right for me, and I'll do it when I'm ready.*

But of course, it's not always that easy, like when a cashier asks you to donate 33 cents to the Children's Hospital fund.

Fredi said that *people tend to get in trouble when they embrace a should that isn't authentic; it stresses them out. The stress comes from clinging to the notion that you should be grateful when you're not, should forgive a person when you don't want to, or that you should be a certain way when you'd rather be another. It's important to pay attention to the stress because that's your body's way of telling you that it isn't happy with your decision.*

I had no doubt this donation thing was stressing me out. My body knew it, but I didn't understand why. The problem was that my *shoulds* all sounded valid to me. I *should* be willing to help a family in need. I *should* donate to a worthwhile charity. I *should* care about people less fortunate than me. I *shouldn't* be making such a fuss over thirty-three cents. I *shouldn't* let something like this stress me out.

These *shoulds* and *shouldn'ts* made sense. They sounded reasonable. So where was the stress coming from?

I pondered this and concluded that I'd donated my thirty-three cents, not because I wanted to, but because I was telling myself I *should* help others in need. And since I knew little Timmy and his gang of dying friends needed help, I felt guilty for not wanting to give. Therefore, since my donation came from a place of guilt, and not from a genuine desire to give, I wasn't being authentic.

Pleased with myself, I told Fredi about my conclusion. She listened, considered my response, and suggested I think about it some more.

I hate when she says things like that... but I kind of love it too. It's sexy. It's like she's challenging me to a duel of wits. It's a challenge to see if I can figure out my dysfunction on my own.

With her gauntlet thrown, the logical gears in my head began to spin.

OK, so my original assumption was that I was donating out of guilt because I should be helping those in need. However, if that were true, I would have donated back in the days when they put those jars next to the cash register, but I didn't. The only time I threw money in those jars was when I wanted to get rid of my change, usually because I was wearing a swimsuit without pockets. Therefore, refusing to help others in need isn't something that bothers me.

Maybe it had something to do with the cashier asking me to help fight cancer. Maybe I was telling myself that a good person should help fight cancer, and I wanted to be a good person. Except, I know I'm a good person, relatively speaking, whether I donate or not. So, this wasn't about me wanting to be a good person... unless I was concerned what everyone else thought of me. If that were true, then that would explain why I was so worried about the cashier and the other customers judging me...

Damn it! That was it! I only donated because I wanted everyone else to think I was a good person! It had nothing to do with helping Timmy or fighting cancer, it was all about me! And as Fredi once mentioned, *if your actions aren't based on being who you are, but instead on how you might appear to others, then what a fantastic basis for being inauthentic.*

Ouch!

So, I took Fredi's advice. I started listening to what my body was telling me rather than what my *shoulds* kept telling me. I stopped donating. It sucked. It felt horrible. Every time I said no, I felt like an ass. But as I began to respect my authentic self, and as I continued to work through my other dysfunctions, things began to change. I stopped shaming myself. It no longer bothered me as much when someone asked me to donate, and I no longer felt resentful when they did. I'd begun to respect my inner truth, and once I did, an interesting thing happened.

Fredi and I attended a benefit event for the Arizona Children's Association (AZCA). Rather than going, I would have preferred to have my teeth drilled, but Fredi was one of AZCA's directors at the time and wanted me to go. The benefit had been the brainchild of a local dance instructor who had adopted a child from AZCA and wanted to give back to the organization that had done so much for him and his family.

Filled with personal stories, fantastic dance routines, and a roadmap of how the money would be spent, both Fredi and I were moved. After concluding the event, the sponsors requested an extra donation, and although we had already paid a hefty sum to attend, Fredi suggested we donate an extra twenty dollars. I told her that I'd take care of it, walked up to the cashier, and handed them a hundred instead.

That moment marked the first time I truly gave to charity. And just like Fredi said, my body knew the difference, because not only did I want to give that day, but I felt damn good for doing it!

9

HIGH SCHOOL SWAT

Our SWAT team's inaugural mission was to capture a homicide suspect out of Las Vegas who was said to be armed, dangerous, and hiding in a house with several known criminals. Investigators believed the suspect was still in possession of the murder weapon and said he had declared his intent to never be taken alive. Intelligence sources had also reported that a methamphetamine lab was in a detached garage next to the home, which isn't a trivial issue to contend with since their toxic fumes can be explosive and fatal if inhaled. The exposure risk to these chemicals is so severe that a fire rescue team is always staged nearby to decontaminate anyone removed from these homes, even if the lab isn't active at the time.

Since two separate structures were involved and would divide our inexperienced team's resources, we called in a second team from an adjoining jurisdiction. They would handle the meth lab while we went after the murder suspect. I had been chosen as the assistant team leader and was specifically tasked with taking a three-man group into the basement of the home where the suspect was believed to be hiding.

As we arrived at our drop-off point, I could feel my heart pounding. Cops were everywhere: K-9 officers preparing their dogs in the event a suspect ran, perimeter officers getting into position with their rifles, and two distinct lines of SWAT team members each headed toward their respective entry points.

Initially, these choreographed movements were made in silence under the cover of darkness, but as we got close, the area erupted into a theater of sound: officers yelling, "Police! Search warrant! Open the door!", barking dogs, shattering glass, detonating flash-bangs, the splintering of a wooden door, and above it all, the sound of my breath being amplified by the filters of my gas mask. I felt like I had a front-row ticket to the greatest show on earth!

In less than a minute and a half from arrival, I was standing over our murder suspect whom I'd ordered to the ground. The operation had gone flawlessly, except for one thing. While walking through the living room, I noticed that my field of view had narrowed. I entered the living room through the front door, which lay scattered in pieces across the entryway, and saw several suspects being forced down by the team members in front of me. I identified the basement door through which I would lead my team, and as I snaked my way through the crowded room, I could tell my field of view had changed. It had narrowed, only slightly, as if the edges had been lightly cropped. The sensation is called tunnel vision and it is a common side effect when one is in a fight or flight situation.

Holding our homicide suspect at gunpoint, I waited for the team leader's announcement that the house had been cleared of threats. As I stood there in the dimly lit room, my mind began reeling. *Fuck, how could this have happened to me? I didn't feel scared, if anything, I felt exhilarated. In fact, if given the chance, I would have called my best friend: "Dude, you won't believe what I'm doing right now!" So, what the hell happened? Did I panic? Was I scared? What if the guys found out about this? Damnit, I'm the assistant team leader for God's sake, what would they think?*

After the investigators arrived and took over the scene, we boarded our bus, and once free from public view, we all began high-fiving and chit-chatting about our first mission. Soon after the bus departed, the interior lights were shut off and the team got quiet. Everyone was reflecting on their part, replaying it in their minds, and there I was in the dark reconciling my thoughts. *SWAT cops shouldn't be afraid, right? Maybe it was just the first-time jitters. Maybe next time it will get better. I mean, damn it, that was so fucking cool, but what if I'm not the right guy for the job, then what?*

I decided that I would tell no one. This would be my secret.

Midway back to the station, our breacher, a well-respected and very large man suddenly let out a hearty laugh and exclaimed, "In all that excitement, I forgot to check the front door to see if it was unlocked and just rammed it instead; I shattered it to pieces!" The inside of the bus then broke out in chatter as several other officers admitted their mishaps, nervousness, and sensory effects like tunnel vision. The excitement of our first hit had gotten to us all.

It should have been no surprise to me that I had a fight-or-flight response. This was by far the biggest mission I'd ever been involved with, and I was seconds away from a possible gunfight with a suspect who had promised not to be taken alive. If anything, my decision to continue the fight by going into the basement was a good one. Had I chosen to turn around in the living room to run back outside, then I might have had cause for concern.

Unfortunately, this realization didn't stick with me. I spent seven years on the team, and I don't think I ever feared getting shot, stabbed, or suffering some other mishap. I did, however, fear on a daily basis that I'd do something to make myself look weak in front of my team. My situation was much like what Franklin D. Roosevelt described when he said, "*The only thing we have to fear, is fear itself.*" I wasn't afraid of going through the door, I was afraid that I'd be afraid of going through the door. I was afraid of even looking afraid.

Unlike the breacher, I wasn't about to admit what happened; I was too afraid of what my teammates would have thought. I'm guessing that the only reason that I and the others confessed to our mishaps was because the breacher had said something first. He was strong in both muscle and character and therefore, if he was fearful or hyped up, it was okay for us to be as well. I'm guessing if one of the weaker members of the team had said something first, the others might have pounced on that person like a pack of wolves and no one would have admitted a thing.

The situation was no different from those I experienced in high school. I was always so careful to choose my words out of fear of what others might think. I'm not sure I was alone in feeling like that, but there were always a couple of kids who didn't seem to care. I'd hear some kid confess that he liked kitty cats, or liked hand lotion for making his skin feel soft, or that he wet his bed throughout junior high school, and I'd stand there in awe. How could he admit that out loud? What was even stranger was that the wolves wouldn't attack. I'd stand there thinking that at any moment I'd see this kid get shredded before my eyes, but nothing ever happened. Stranger still, some of these alarmingly honest kids were kind of ordinary and even nerdy. It seemed like these kids could be found in any one of the social groups, and they didn't seem to care to which group they'd been assigned.

I was sure I was one of the losers, and I was also sure that losers were the only ones who felt insecure. It never occurred to me that some of the cheerleaders or football players might have felt the same way. I mean, why wouldn't they fear they weren't cool enough, pretty enough, strong enough, smart enough, or skilled enough? I'm guessing some of those jocks who duct-taped the butt cheeks of kids together only did so to create a bigger-looking loser than they themselves felt. And more than likely, some of those stuck-up cheerleaders, who turned up their noses to anyone who wasn't in their inner circle, were terrified to be seen with the average student for fear they would be branded uncool. These kids, whom I'd perceived as popular, were walking the same tightrope I was, desperately trying to control what others thought of them by carefully choosing their every word and action.

Come to think of it, I bet just about everyone in those high school hallways spent time worrying about what others thought. We all wanted to be acknowledged and liked and not be put down or made to look stupid. Some of us were trying our best to go through the day and not be called clumsy, stupid, ugly, or fat, while others were doing their best to get called beautiful, strong, or powerful. This latter group needed praise to reassure themselves of their superior status because, without it, they felt like their popularity was waning.

This was an odd concept for me to ponder, that those who strive to succeed because they need praise to feel good, are just as dysfunctional as those who allow criticism to make them feel bad. It's like everyone in those high school hallways was dependent on the opinion of others to define their worth. Everyone except for those few kids who didn't seem to care. Those kids knew who they were, regardless of what others thought. They didn't need to be complimented, nor did they care if they were criticized, which left them free to be themselves.

I'd spent the majority of my life attempting to get others to believe I was the man I wanted to be. I wanted them to know I was strong, confident, and brave. But if anything happened that tarnished that image, I got all freaked out. I felt like I had to be perfect, and it only got worse when I became the SWAT team leader.

One day, our team was in a training room that we built to practice breaching doors and entering rooms to clear them. The team was eating lunch, and I thought it would be funny to leap through the window and surprise them while yelling, "Police, nobody move!" Dressed in full tactical gear, I ran to the window as fast as I could, planted my hand on the window ledge, swung my legs up, and totally failed to clear the opening. In other words, I ran full speed into the side of the training house while shouting something indiscernible before falling back into a cloud of dust. They laughed, I laughed, but behind my laughter was humiliation.

It didn't matter whether I had done a hundred things correctly, or whether they had just finished telling me I had awesome tactical skills, shooting abilities, or had put together a great training day. If I thought I had done the slightest thing wrong, my day was shot. And that's the problem with insecurity; it's so caustic that I didn't even have to do anything wrong, I'd just see a couple of guys laughing and automatically assume they were laughing at me.

I might have looked like a SWAT Team Leader, and I might have actually been one, but on the inside, I still felt like the same loser I was in high school.

10

YOU MADE ME ANGRY

The affair with my mistress had gone on for about three months when she decided it was time to come clean to her husband. Knowing that word of our affair would spread quickly, I didn't have much choice but to tell my wife as well. I had already decided to leave her, but I didn't want her to know that. I figured it would soften the blow if she thought I was confused, still loved her, and was having a difficult time myself. But after I confessed, my desire to move on overshadowed any need for compassion, and so within a day of admitting my infidelity, I was ready to move out. I told her I needed to be on my own to reflect on the situation and promptly packed my bags to leave.

As I walked out of my house for the final time, I felt nothing: no sorrow, no sadness, not even a tinge of guilt. Meanwhile, my wife was chasing after me while trying to comprehend these rapid-fire events that were destroying her marriage. Having played the role of the perfect husband all along, her emotional sensors and scanners were desperately reaching out to me, trying to re-establish a connection, but there was nothing there.

So, as she pleaded after me to stay and talk, I left without turning back. This was perhaps the most baffling part for her; what happened to her husband and why wasn't he responding as he'd always done before?

The truth is, I didn't leave her that night, I left her a long time before that. I'd been asleep. I'd been operating on autopilot. I'd been playing the role of a loving husband by doing all the things a loving husband should do, but it was all an act designed to make my friends, my family, my wife, and perhaps even myself think I was a good husband. I don't think I was consciously trying to fool anyone; I'd just been doing what I should. But once I had the affair and the decision to leave was made, there was no more reason to continue the act, so I simply walked off stage.

Having become aware of my insecurities, I looked back at this earlier time to understand why this had happened. I had been married to a woman whom I once called my best friend, who gave birth to my only son, and then proceeded to leave her without feeling a thing. Was that even possible? Probably not.

I think I only believed I felt nothing because I was good at stuffing and hiding my emotions. I was an expert at ignoring anything that even resembled one. I only remember feeling something about my ex-wife once, and it happened six months after I walked out the door. It was a feeling so deep that a single tear welled up in my eye and rolled down my cheek. I'm not being sarcastic either. I never cried about anything, not even my mother's funeral.

The tear came when my soon-to-be ex-wife and I sat in a dimly lit courtroom waiting to be divorced. There were no lawyers, legal assistants, or witnesses, it was just the judge and the two of us. She was seated in the front row of a dozen or so empty pews on her side of the courtroom, while I sat across the aisle in my own set of empty pews. As the judge read the divorce decree out loud, I turned and looked at the woman with whom I'd spent the last ten years. All alone, and without family or friends to support her, I watched as she quietly sobbed into a handkerchief. As if sensing my gaze, she slowly turned and looked at me. We stayed like that for several minutes, eyes locked, and that's when I felt a surge of emotion begin to grow along my spine. It was a tingling sensation that continued to build and radiate throughout my body until it cracked through my emotional armor, allowing that single tear to flow.

The two of us had shared a lot of memories, and some part of me was heartbroken to see it end.

There was, however, another feeling in me, not in the courtroom, but during that same time. It was a feeling that I was curiously unaware of. Anger. I was pissed off. I had been telling my friends during those years that my wife was such a bitch. She was so selfish and always had to have everything her way. "She's like a Mack truck," I used to say, "running me over to get whatever the hell she wants; and why is it always me that has to give in?"

It wasn't just a little anger; it was a lot. But where did it come from, and was it really her fault? I didn't know it at the time, but the anger wasn't caused by her, it had come from me. It came as a result of my philosophies. It came from my code of chivalry and honor. It came from the fact that I was in control of my emotions and didn't let anything bother me. It came from being married to a woman for almost 10 years and pretending everything was okay when it wasn't. It came from the fact that I had completely failed to deal with my problems and all the irritations that had accumulated inside of me.

It came because, I hadn't been processing my emotions, I'd been swallowing and stuffing them instead. Unbeknownst to me, if you swallow your anger, resentment, and frustration, it doesn't go away. It just sits in your belly and festers. And the more you swallow, the more it collects, and the bigger and nastier it gets. I was furious at her because I had collected 10 years' worth of shit and kept swallowing it until it had become a giant ball of rage.

As a cop, I used to see this pattern evolve a lot in neighborhood disputes. We'd show up at these calls, and the involved parties would either be screaming profanities and threats at each other or would already be entangled in a vicious brawl. We'd separate the combatants only to discover that the source of the dispute was something trivial; that a dog had peed on a rosebush, that one neighbor had run his lawn mower six inches into the other's yard, or that a sprinkler had watered the back of a neighbors shed. How could such a small event cause such a dramatic reaction between two mature adults?

I believe these fights happened, not because a little dog named Sparky had peed on the neighbor's rosebush, but because Sparky had been peeing on the rosebush for the last six months. The first time the rose bush owner saw it happen, it angered him, but he decided not to address it. He told himself that it was only a little bit of dog pee, and therefore hardly an issue worth getting upset about. Besides, he didn't want to be one of those neighbors who complained about every little thing. So, he ignored it and decided not to let it bother him. In other words, he swallowed his anger.

However, this approach doesn't work, and so his irritation and anger didn't go away. It was still there. And each day that Sparky peed on the bush, a little more anger got swallowed and deposited, but the neighbor continued not to say anything because the circumstances hadn't changed. If he complained about it now, he'd still be complaining about just a little pee.

As time passed, the rosebush began to reek of urine, and the surrounding grass began to yellow and die. And as the man's anger continued to grow, he started to villainize his neighbor.

"How in the hell can he keep allowing this to happen?" he asks his wife, "I would never allow my dog to behave like this, never! But apparently, he doesn't care, after all, it's not his rose bush that's getting destroyed. I swear, the nerve of some people! I mean, that guy has got to be the biggest and most inconsiderate jackass in this entire god-damn neighborhood!"

And so, once the bush dies, the owner finally decides to address the issue. And when he does, he unloads six months of collected anger onto his unsuspecting neighbor who now feels ambushed, defensive, and wrongly accused.

And this is how two mature adults get into a fistfight over a dog that peed on a rosebush.

I didn't realize it, but just like the owner of the rosebush, I hadn't been honest with myself or my first wife, and I had failed to deal with my shit. I had all these reasons for not saying anything. I told myself that I was a chivalrous man and should always let my wife choose the restaurant we went to. But each time I did, I swallowed a little bit of anger and resentment while trying to excuse the feeling away as an honorable deed. And each time I let her choose where we spent our Christmas holiday or where we went on vacation, I was swallowing a little bit more. And on those few occasions when I tried to stand up for what I wanted but surrendered when she started to beg, those were the days I guzzled down the anger. And even though I agreed to all these dinners and trips and demands, the anger was still there, and dammit, someone had to be responsible for making me feel that way! It was her fault! She's such a bitch!.

I was blaming her for something I'd been doing to myself. And the more I reflected on this, the more examples of collected anger I began to uncover. And it wasn't just limited to her.

I was angry at all the cashiers who made me donate my change to the Children's Hospital Fund, but I was the one agreeing to donate. I was angry at my supervisor for taking credit for my ideas, but never directly addressed the issue with her. I was angry at the team leader who was undermining my leadership, yet never asked him to stop. I was angry at the police department for their backstabbing management style but never chose to leave and work someplace else. I was angry when my dad showed up late each year for Thanksgiving, which led us to eat cold turkey, but I was the one choosing to wait.

I always had an excuse for not dealing with these issues. I'd minimize both the problem and my anger, and then articulate some kind of perceived righteous reason for not addressing it. *I can't believe the other team leader told the SWAT guys that I worry too much about the details, now I feel like a jackass. But what the hell, he was just teasing me. Besides, if I address it now, the guys on the team will end up joking about it behind my back. They'll say something like, "Ooh, Prochoda's a little grumpy today, better get him a doughnut!" Whatever! It's not a big deal. I just won't let it bother me...*

And that's what I kept telling myself: I just won't let it bother me. But it was bothering me. I know it bothered me because I was constantly bitching and complaining about these things that happened to me. I thought about these issues for days and wouldn't let them go. And the more that these things bothered me, the more my anger became their fault.

This pattern of excusing and minimizing and then failing to do anything about it was adding up and collectively pissing me off. I mean, of course I was unhappy! My boss was a backstabber, my teammate was an undermining bastard, my wife was a selfish bitch, my dad was a disrespectful ass, and there I was in the middle doing nothing to address these issues. But why would I? It wasn't bothering me! And that worked.

It worked because I had them to blame. It was their fault I was angry and unhappy. *I mean, of course I'm unhappy, I'm surrounded by a bunch of selfish assholes who don't give a shit that they're screwing up my life. I'm bending over backward to accommo-date them and just look at what they do to me in return!*

I was convinced I was a nice guy, a guy who didn't make mountains out of molehills, a guy who was willing to take some hits in the spirit of getting along, but who was I really?

An angry and resentful victim of my very own failure to act.

11

THE BOUNDARY

The fact that I'd been responsible for so much of my anger was perhaps the hardest and single most difficult thing I had to wrap my mind around. The problem was that I'd spent nearly a half-century blaming everyone else for my anger, and that made sense to me. It was logical. It was an example of cause and effect in its purest form. *You said or did this, which made me angry, therefore, you made me angry.* Duh! Obvious! No more need for discussion! Case closed!

Unfortunately, Fredi calls this a victim mentality and wouldn't let me close my case. She said, "*If you're going to let other people control how you feel, then go right ahead. But I refuse to give someone else that kind of power over me.*"

Her point was that it's okay to be angry and that anger is a healthy emotion to express when we've been wronged, but the choice to be angry is ours alone. No one else controls that.

"Well, what about when someone cuts me off in traffic?" I asked, "That pisses me off!"

"So, you're going to let that person, a complete stranger, spoil the rest of your day?"

"Well, what am I supposed to do? He's driving like a jackass! Of course that's going to piss me off!"

"And you're going to let that spoil your day?"

"Look honey, if someone drives like a jackass and cuts me off in traffic, that's gonna piss me off. I'm not built like you; I can't let that go."

"So, then what? You're going to flip him off? Maybe run him off the road? Get into a fistfight? What's that going to get you?"

"It'll teach him a lesson. It will make him think twice about doing it again."

"And that will make you feel better?"

"Yesss!"

"What if he doesn't care that you're pissed off? What if he just flips you off in return? What if he wins the fight or you get arrested? Then how will you feel?"

"Honey, that's just who I am. I can't control who I am."

"Bullshit! That's just who you're choosing to be. You aren't pissed off because he cut you off in traffic, you're pissed off because he isn't behaving the way you *think* he should."

"Damn straight!" I replied, "He's behaving like a jackass!"

"The problem is that you can't control what other people think, or do, or how they behave. So, if you go around getting pissed off at all these people doing all these things that you have no control over, then you're just setting yourself up for failure—you'll always be pissed off!"

I didn't want to admit it, but she was right. And the truth was, I was pissed off. I was pissed off at the police department for their management style, their ethics, and the candidates they chose to promote. I was pissed off at people who tried to push their values onto me, for the political candidates they chose to elect, and for the decisions those candidates later made. I was pissed off at the newscasters who reported things I thought should remain private, at the paparazzi who

harassed the Hollywood stars, and at athletes who were paid
outrageous salaries that made game tickets unaffordable. I was
pissed off at vendors who sold shitty products, video games
requiring in-game purchases to win, and tax breaks and
discounts given to mega-corporations that suck money out of
local economies.

I spent countless hours being angry about things over which
I had no control. And what did all that anger get me? Nothing.
My anger wasn't driving change. These people and companies
didn't care whether I was angry; most of the time they didn't
even know I existed. Fredi was right; getting pissed off was doing
nothing but making me miserable.

However, there was only one problem. All these things were
pissing me off! So, how could I stop feeling that way? I mean,
you can't swallow your anger, it just stays there and festers in
your belly, so what the hell was I supposed to do?

Fredi explained it like this: *Getting angry is a habit. Something
happens, and we let our emotions take over. You've got to slow the
process down; slow it down and ask yourself what you're upset about.
You're upset because some entity is doing something you wouldn't do
or that you don't agree with, but it's something over which you have
no direct control. You've got to stop and realize that you can't control
the decisions that other people make, and this is difficult to do because
we try so hard to control others, control what they think, control what
they do, control what they say, but we can't. All we can do is choose
how we respond. We can choose to let them make us angry, demoralize us, or destroy us, or we can choose to realize that some things are
simply out of our control. As they say, "shit happens", and that's just
the reality of life.*

Choosing to focus on how I responded to a situation rather
than how I felt about it would become one of the most powerful
concepts she would impart to me. It's so powerful because it
requires me to focus on what I can control, rather than getting

upset over what I can't. It would also be my first exposure to what the term *"having boundaries"* truly means.

For those who may not be familiar with boundaries, allow me to rewind into my past. I was pissed off at my first wife because she made dinner plans without consulting me first. I didn't want to have dinner with the neighbors because I wanted to stay home and relax. However, I felt compelled to go because the neighbors were expecting us and had already prepared our meal. Then, my wife did it again, and again, and again, and although I complained each time, she kept doing it.

So, there I was getting pissed off over something I couldn't control, my wife making dinner plans without asking me first, without focusing on what I could control, which was whether I went to dinner. My wife was not taking my complaints seriously because she always got her way. It didn't matter whether she asked me or not; I continued to come along. What I needed to say was, "It makes me angry when you make plans without asking me first, so, because I get to control my schedule, I'll agree to come along this time, but if you don't ask me next time, I may not be joining you."

I just had to clarify my boundaries and let her face the natural consequences of her decision. In other words, let her explain to the neighbors why I'm not there. Let her feel the awkwardness of the neighbors cooking too much food. Let her feel the disappointment of eating alone with another couple. And by sharing my intent ahead of time, she couldn't claim I put her in an awkward position, because the responsibility would fall on her shoulders, and hers alone. By going to dinner when I didn't want to, I'd been letting her walk over my boundaries and had absorbed a lot of anger and resentment because of it.

The same thing was happening with my dad at Thanksgiving. It had become a family norm that I hosted Thanksgiving at my house, and every year my dad would show up late leading all of us to eat cold turkey. I justified waiting for my dad by telling myself that families should eat together because that's the way we were raised. But just like with my ex-wife, I wasn't upholding my boundaries. Instead, I was *should'ing* myself. He was the one being disrespectful for being late, not me, so I finally told him, "When you fail to show up for dinner on time, we all end up waiting and the food gets cold, so, if you aren't on time next year, we'll be starting without you. I do hope you come early."

It's like, I'd been taking on the problem of him being late, but now I was giving it back. And it worked; he's been on time ever since. By approaching the problem this way, I wasn't requiring him to change and therefore there was no need for an argument. He was still free to show up whenever he wanted, I just informed him what would happen if he was late.

Because eating together was a family norm, my brain never considered the option of starting without him. It just seemed wrong. Yet, for those who were raised without similar expectations, this whole scenario likely seems rather obvious. Unfortunately, that's often the reality of boundaries; everyone can see the problem but you.

However, once I began to understand my boundary issues, and pay attention to when I felt irritated, I got better at fixing them. My son learned if he wasn't ready for school on time then he'd have to change out of his pajamas in the school parking lot. My boss learned that I would no longer agree to work the unfilled shift every time he asked and that he would need to ask other people. When Fredi cut off our cable TV, thus enforcing a boundary to stop watching the news, I learned how these stations excel at creating negative emotions. All they did was expose me to thousands of stories that were making me angry but over which I had virtually no control. With no news, the world felt like it became a better place overnight.

But while these boundaries were changing my life, there was

still one case in which they had no effect. It was those damn drivers who kept cutting me off in traffic. I needed to find a way to keep from getting angry, but it seemed that I had few options. If they were driving recklessly, I could call the police and file a report, and if they got too close to the front of my car, I could honk my horn. But those solutions weren't helping, I was still shaking my fist and yelling obscenities at my windshield.

I needed to look at my anger to figure out why I was choosing it. I wondered whether it was because these erratic drivers were forcing me to take action by slamming on my brakes, but I never got upset when I slammed on my brakes to avoid a squirrel or a rabbit. Then I considered whether it was the act of getting cut off that was making me angry, but I never got angry when driving in big cities where cutting off other drivers is the norm. I also didn't get angry when someone swerved in and back out of my lane because I knew they hadn't seen me.

This left me with only one conclusion. It must have been the driver's intent that was pissing me off. It was the disrespect that they were showing me. It was me saying, *You bastard! I can't believe you just did that to me!*

But is that really what was happening, or was that just a story I was telling myself? Because when I consider the times that I've cut off other drivers off, it wasn't personal...

I was just late.

12

BURNT HASHBROWNS

The first time Fredi told me that she had fired a patient for failing to do the tasks listed on their agreed-upon treatment plan, I was taken aback.

"You're a doctor, aren't you supposed to help?" I asked.

"I am helping, but they aren't doing their part. If they don't do what they've agreed to do, then why should I waste my time? I can use that appointment to work with someone else, someone who's willing to do the work necessary to help themselves."

"Yeah, but they still need your help, and you're a doctor."

"If they aren't willing to do what's needed to improve their situation, then I'm just banging my head against the wall. It's not like I can force them to do it, it's up to them. Besides, if I don't require them to do their part, I'm reinforcing the idea that someone else is responsible for fixing them. And that's simply not true."

It didn't seem right. I figured a medical provider was bound by a code of ethics that directed them to help those in need, but did that make sense?

I saw a similar issue as a cop when dealing with alcoholics and drug addicts. I'd refer them to various services, but if they weren't interested, it didn't help. We'd throw them in detox, but as soon as they got out, they'd be right back at it again.

Over a period of years, I'd get called back to these residences regularly, and these repeated visits would stitch together in my mind like a time-lapse photography film. As if watching a video of a flower that rapidly sprouts and dies, I saw a similar transformation in these folks as their health declined, their relationships crumbled, and their finances dwindled to nothing. It seemed that no amount of help made a difference; they had to reach their low point before things would change. Sometimes they made miraculous recoveries, and sometimes they died, but ultimately, the choice was theirs.

Fredi was right. You can't help someone who isn't willing to do the work required to change their circumstance, so why waste your time? If people want to get better, they need to play a part in their recovery.

She used similar boundaries with patients who were late. Her standing policy was that if her patients showed up more than ten minutes past their scheduled appointment, it would be marked as a missed visit and they would be rescheduled. And if they failed to show up a second time, then they'd be referred to another provider.

"Aren't you being kind of harsh with your office policies?" I asked, "Sometimes people really do have a flat tire."

"That's why I give them two chances", she said with a smile. Then she clarified, "Look, my schedule slips when I have a late patient. I plan my day so that I have enough time to assess my patients, which is why I won't cut my visits short; I refuse to give substandard care. If a patient shows up late, then the next patient won't be seen on time, and that's not fair to them. And if that keeps happening, then my staff and I work late and miss breaks and that's not fair to us. Therefore, if I allow someone to disregard my office policies, I'm allowing them to disrespect my time, the time of my staff, and the time of my other patients. Besides, I don't need the stress of a schedule that's always running late because that's how providers get burned out."

She went on to explain that good boundaries also teach her patients good habits and are a sign of respect. Having been raised poor, Fredi noticed that people who work with that population often treat them as if they are incapable of being polite, incapable of having good manners, incapable of being clean, and incapable of respecting other people. As a young girl, she felt marginalized when she was treated as if she were incapable, and certainly didn't appreciate it. As she puts it, "Expecting someone to be respectful, and therefore capable of improvement, is a form of respect in itself."

She admits that asserting her boundaries isn't always easy, since some people confronted with them get angry. It feels unfair when they're denied service because they can't get away with something that they have before. This potential for confrontation is often a major reason why people don't like enforcing their boundaries because sometimes, it's easier to give in than to hold one's ground. Another reason people don't uphold their boundaries is that they reframe their non-enforcement of a boundary as an act of kindness done in the spirit of helping the other person out. Bending the rules doesn't help anyone she notes; it just adds to the confusion by changing the expectations of what is allowed, thereby reinforcing bad habits.

Her words reminded me of a time when I had developed a pattern of paying my rent late. I never considered it a problem since I always had an excuse to get out of late fees. A few months after moving into an apartment in Denver, I received a notice of late rent the day after it was due. The notice demanded full rent along with an extra fifty dollars in late fees.

The apartment complex was managed by these two sweet old ladies, and I couldn't believe they would charge me fifty bucks for being one day late. So, I filled out a check, without late fees of course, and scribbled in the prior week's date. I walked into the office, placed my check on the counter, and explained that I had intended to bring the rent earlier but had forgotten because the check had slipped off my desk. With an apologetic smile, I explained that I was sure they could appreciate how this might have happened, and therefore expected them to waive my late fees. They listened, smiled, pointed to my lease, and promptly demanded their fifty bucks.

After some discussion, I realized they wouldn't concede. I reached for the checkbook in my back pocket, the same one I'd intentionally left at home, and feigned surprise when I couldn't find it. I expressed my sincerest apologies and suggested that perhaps to avoid any inconvenience, they might consider excusing my late fees just this one time. With a friendly smile, they assured me that waiting for their 50 bucks was no inconvenience at all.

Crotchety old bitches, I thought as I walked home to get my checkbook, *nothing but a pair of penny-pinching hags!*

Fredi was right. If you always give someone a break, they'll never learn to be on time. I didn't respect any of my previous landlords for giving me a break; I was just glad that they did. As for those two old hags, I may have thought they were bitches, but that was the last time my rent was late.

Stories like this are why I love living with Fredi; she teaches me things. I get to watch her interact with the world almost every day. I get to ask her questions, hear her opinions, and share my stories to see what she thinks. These daily interactions provide me with little clues and glimpses into dysfunctional behaviors that happen all the time.

We'll be sitting in a restaurant, and I'll notice Fredi has no hesitation in sending her burnt hashbrowns back to the kitchen. I never do that; I worry too much about what the cook might do to my food. One of my cop buddies told me he was eating ice from a soda cup when he noticed a glob of phlegm stuck to the bottom of his cup. The two kids working the fast-food counter that day later regretted their decision to spit in his cup, but the thought of finding something like that in my food still haunts me to this day. I told Fredi the story, thinking she might reconsider sending her food back, and she looked up at me, dumbfounded.

"I won't keep my mouth shut," she replied, "they burnt my hash browns! The cook knows he burnt them, the person preparing my plate could see they were burnt, and so did the waitress who brought them out to me. Yet, all three of them decided to serve them anyway. Screw that! I don't care if they don't like it; they can cook me up a fresh batch."

So, as Fredi is handed her freshly cooked plate of hash browns, the waitress turns to me and asks how I like my breakfast just as I bite down on a piece of bacon that shatters between my teeth. Quickly swallowing the burnt shards and charcoaled remains, I give her a thumbs up and respond, "Perfect, tastes great! Thanks for asking!"

It's Fredi's clarity on these matters that I value. While so many people ignore and accept these indiscretions into their lives, Fredi doesn't. Instead, she stands up and says *bullshit*. She's not afraid of confrontation, and she's not afraid to hold back just because she's worried some cook might spit in her food. If that were to happen, she'd deal with it, but as she points out, the more that people refuse to accept sub-standard food, the less inclined the wait staff will be to serve it in the first place.

She's got a point... I like the way she thinks.

13

THE MANY FACES OF FEAR

When I was a boy, I used to play for hours with my Matchbox cars. I'd choreograph wicked car chases, massive accidents, and spectacular jumps into the sides of domino built skyscrapers that roared as they came crashing down. Among my favorite of these vehicles was a little red van that had lights and sirens on top. Originally an ambulance, I'd pulled off the stickers and, using my best penmanship, had carefully written "S.W.A.T." on both sides. Even back then I knew what I wanted to be when I grew up.

I loved being on SWAT, which is why deciding to retire from the team was perhaps one of the hardest decisions I'd ever made. I spent seven years on that team, helping to build it from scratch, and SWAT had become not only a part of my life but a part of my identity.

My retirement began when the commander presented me with an engraved plaque and a picture drawn by renowned tactical artist Dick Kramer that had been signed by the members of my team. The commander then outlined my accomplishments and highlighted several notable missions we had completed together, and as I stood there next to him, I tried but couldn't stop the tears from welling up. I was going to miss these guys.

After the ceremony, the commander invited us out to lunch where he challenged us with his SWAT coin. This coin, inscribed with the team crest and motto, is given to new members who are expected to always carry it with them. By throwing his coin onto the table, the commander was calling on all of us to do the same. As the rules of this challenge go, if everyone has their coin, the challenger buys dinner and drinks for all, but for any who can't produce their coin on the spot, the entire bill is transferred to them. I had mine ready, as they knew I would. We'd all been reminded of the importance of carrying our coins by a former teammate who was forced to pay for his own retirement party after forgetting his coin in his car. As we ate, drank, and laughed together, I reflected on how fortunate I had been to work with these guys. I had entrusted them with my life, and they had never let me down.

After lunch, I returned to the police department where I found my desk covered with a pile of my personally owned tactical gear. This wasn't SWAT tradition; this was bullshit.

Storming into the watch commander's office, I confronted the new team leader.

"Who the fuck dumped my gear all over my desk, and why is half my shit missing?"

"Whoa! Calm down Prochoda. I did it. I told a couple of the guys to empty your bags so we could give your department-owned gear to the new guy."

"Well, fuck you, then. Nobody touches my gear. Go find the rest of my shit."

Seeming a bit surprised at the magnitude of my anger, he reiterated that he was just trying to bring the new guy on board as soon as possible. However, seeing that my clenched jaw was the only response he would get, he left in search of the other officers who later returned my gear and apologized for the misunderstanding.

I'm guessing that the new team leader knew why I was angry about having my property dumped on my desk, especially when he learned that some of it was missing. He may have even understood why leaving the team was emotional for me, and that letting me empty my bags may have helped me process my separation. However, what I think continued to baffle him was the magnitude of my anger and my absolute refusal to forgive him.

I understood his confusion, after all, he didn't have all the facts.

What the new team leader didn't know, and what I never told him, was that mixed into my pile of gear was a single OB brand tampon. Lacking the conventional insertion device, the OB tampon is much smaller than a standard one and resembles a plastic-wrapped bullet. The tampon had not been set on top of my belongings like a flagpole, nor had it been loaded into one of my pistol magazines, nor had anyone drawn a smiley face on it to resemble a tiny SWAT officer standing at attention. Instead, the tampon simply lay there, no more noticeable than any other item on my desk.

The reason for this random placement is not because my teammates had placed it there to make fun of me, but because the tampon belonged to me. I'd carried it in my supply pouch on the front of my vest since my earliest days on the team, and it had simply been dumped out of my pouch along with all my other gear. I carried it because a paramedic once told me that tampons work great for plugging bullet wounds. I carried it because I thought that one day, I might use it to save a life.

I also carried a wire saw that could be used to cut a branch or a section of wooden fence, a small hand mirror that was mounted on an extendable rod that could be used to look around corners, and a multi-use tool that would have come in handy when disassembling an electrical panel or a locking mechanism. I carried these items because I imagined that someday they might come in useful and that, thanks to my keen foresight, I would have been prepared to handle the situation. But that day never arrived, and now, as I looked at these items, I no longer felt like a SWAT Team leader, but like a fucking boy scout.

These items embarrassed me. I felt childish for having carried them. I shuddered to think what my teammates might have said when they saw them. Had they laughed and made fun of me? Had they speculated that I carried the tampon in the unlikely event that I got my period just as I was about to kick in a door? Did they parade this little plastic bullet around the office, showing everyone what they found in Prochoda's SWAT bag while simulating how I might have tactically squatted to insert it while covering a suspect with my gun?

I was humiliated.

I was furious at the new team leader for having invaded my privacy. I was angry at him for having revealed my hidden stash of tools. He had not only embarrassed me on my final day on SWAT but had condemned me to a legacy for which I would henceforth be known: *Prochoda – the tampon-toting Boy Scout warrior.*

Without knowing it, the new team leader subjected me to a disrespect that had been entirely created and experienced within the confines of my own head. And I'm quite certain of this fact because I never once heard any mention of a Boy Scout warrior, a tampon, or any other reference to the items found in my bag that day.

The fear of losing my team's respect, a fear that had plagued me throughout my time on SWAT, had entirely dictated my response. This fear had not only tarnished my last day but had created a rift between me and the new team leader that possibly exists to this day. However, none of that mattered to me at the time because having him think I was an asshole was far better than admitting the truth.

The new team leader might have thought he'd been interacting with me that day, but he hadn't. He'd been interacting with the face of my fears. And this hadn't been the first time.

The SWAT guys used to call me ice-cold, a fact for which I was immensely proud. They'd point at my face after a serious incident and say, "Look at Prochoda, nothing ever shakes him... nothing." I was proud when they said this because it demonstrated that I had the fortitude and strength to handle even the greatest of adversities. Or, at least, that's what I kept telling myself.

Unfortunately, the authentic me knew the truth. I wasn't ice cold. I was scared. I was scared of screwing up and looking weak in front of the team. I had been feeling things all along but had been stuffing those emotions and swallowing them since childhood. So, as I attempted to convince myself that I was mentally tough, the real me was feeling ashamed for feeling so weak. And since I thought the real me and my tough exterior were the same thing, these conflicting feelings created a lot of tension and drama inside that only served to further increase my fears. Unfortunately, more fear necessitates more control, which in turn creates more anxiety, thus reinforcing a dysfunctional loop that has no end.

This is why fear is so devastating; it continuously builds on top of itself. It keeps growing bigger and bigger until a person loses perspective of reality. What was I so afraid of anyway? That the SWAT guys might discover that I was a little nervous or excited when we participated in a dangerous mission. That they might see I was a little embarrassed if I screwed up or fantasized about saving a life with a tampon? I had developed this crazy notion that I had to be perfect in every way. My fears had removed any margin of error and had left me walking a tightrope, requiring me to constantly expend tons of energy in a frantic effort to maintain a completely unrealistic set of expectations.

Knowing how deep these fears were rooted in me, and how up until now they controlled much of my life, I started to become aware of the fear in others. It was like I could see fear. Realizing just how much pressure and stress these fears induced in me, I found I was becoming more sympathetic and less judgmental of others and their fears. I understood what these people were going through and how awful they must feel inside.

Fear is like a drug addiction. It's easy to get high and push back the fear the first few times, but it takes more and more to satisfy the craving once the addiction takes hold. When I first began dating one of my two "perfect women", hearing them say that they loved me was all that I needed to feel better. It was easy. But as my insecurities kicked in and took hold, I needed more and more reassurance to feel that the relationship was not in jeopardy. I needed these women to tell me that they not only loved me but loved me more than anyone they'd been with. I needed them to stop talking to guys, to stay at home, and to stop answering the phone. The fear just kept building until I lost perspective and could no longer believe that they still loved me.

They could see my fear, and would even point it out to me, but I was in denial. And much like the drug addict can't stop getting high until he reaches rock bottom, a fearful person does much the same thing. The plastic surgeon can tell the aging movie actress that there is no more skin on her face left to stretch, but until she can acknowledge her distorted features, she won't be able to ignore that little spot next to her chin that looks like the start of a wrinkle and must therefore be destroyed.

Years ago, I knew a dentist who dated the most jealous and

verbally abusive woman. The years of anger within her had soured even her looks. He, on the other hand, was a good-looking man, funny, athletic, and smart, and I wondered why he continued to endure this woman's wrath. Meanwhile, a beautiful woman had fallen in love with him. She was a friend of mine, and I encouraged their affair to help him break free of his current relationship. The two of them seemed made for each other, and although they had fallen deeply in love, he chose to break up with her and remain with the angry woman.

I couldn't comprehend his decision. I kept prodding him for an answer. I needed to understand the insanity that drove him to choose torture over love. Finally, he confessed. The relationship with his lover would never work because of his tiny penis.

"She doesn't care about that; she loves you!"

It was no use. He couldn't hear me. As far as he was concerned, he was unlovable.

I began to think about all the movies I'd watched where a group of women giggled about a date gone bad while repre-senting the measurement of the man's tiny penis with their fingers. I considered all the adult magazines I'd read that contained advertisements for pills and pumps that promised to enlarge a man's erection so he could finally satisfy his lover. I reflected on all the times I'd personally teased male friends that they must of had a *little dick* because they refused some kind of a challenge, while never considering that, maybe they did. And had I said something like that to my friend at an earlier time?

Fifty percent of men have a penis that is smaller than the median size; that's one out of two. How many of them feel unlov-able just like my friend? How many of them are ashamed to be seen at a urinal or while undressing before a potential mate? I understood why my friend was fearful but I felt sad he couldn't comprehend that his fear was unwarranted. This woman loved him, with all her heart, yet because of his fear, they would never be as one.

I have another friend who is funny, smart, insightful, and fun to talk to, but thinks he is unlovable because of his weight. And yet another who is an amazing and gifted carpenter, having built stunning mansions worth millions of dollars, but feels inadequate and stupid because he dropped out of school in 8th grade. These men constantly limit themselves with roadblocks they've built using their distorted perceptions. They flog themselves over perceived flaws that are insignificant in comparison to the magnificent men that they are, just like I had. I feel compassion and offer support, but it's not a battle I can fight. They've got to win that one on their own.

While the faces of fear that these men wore are the types that demoralize people and tear them down, I'm not so sure that they are the hardest types of fear to identify. We know these fears through personal experience or by having witnessed them in others close to us. We are told of these fears in self-help books, by motivational speakers, and in catchy slogans that serve to address them.

But fear has many faces.

In acknowledging my fear, I began to understand fear. I could see how dysfunctional it was and how it drove wildly different behaviors. Fear is not only found in those who believe they are losers but also in those desperate to remain winners. I could see little Miss Smarty Pants and her long list of straight A's driven by a fear that a single B would mark her as a failure. I could see the gay-bashing speeches by the charismatic church leader who was terrified his homosexuality might be discovered. I could see the fear in the doping athlete who felt compelled to cheat because his life had no meaning without his championship title. I used to judge these people so harshly, but now I was starting to understand.

I began to wonder about the others I had judged in the past. Was that cut-throat billionaire really so greedy, or was he just afraid of being named a 'loser' at the yacht club if his company didn't make the Forbes 500? Was that gang banger who said "What the fuck are you looking at" really such a badass, or was he just frightened of looking weak, which in his world makes him the next logical victim? Was that super-friendly guy really that helpful, or was he just afraid that if he refused a request for assistance, he'd be perceived as an unworthy soul on judgment day? Was that woman really that kinky and wild, or was she afraid that if she denied her boyfriend's twisted requests in bed, she'd be unworthy of love?

While I felt compassion for my friends and their various issues, my reactions to these last four had been much different. There was no sympathy for their fears and the misery that they might have felt, only the judgment of how I perceived them. That's because I never paused to consider that, maybe it wasn't them I was judging, but the face of their fear.

14

ME BIG MAN, ME WEAR BIG CONDOM

I used to constantly hear a voice in my head, however, I didn't think of it as a voice, I just thought it was my brain doing its thing. For example, my boss would ask me if I would work an extra shift because someone called in sick, and the voice would start chattering.

Well, I was going to go home and watch TV, but what would my boss think if I said no? He'd think I wasn't a team player. But why does he always ask me? Why doesn't he ever ask John? John never works late. In fact, the one time he did ask John, John responded, "Screw that, I'm going home!" What kind of bullshit reply is that? The boss didn't even blink an eye! But that's the problem. The boss doesn't care. He just asks me. But why me? This is the third time this month and I already said yes the other two times. But if I tell him he should ask John, he'll think I'm just trying to pawn it off on someone else. Crap, I better do it. At least I'll get paid overtime and that way they can't say I'm not willing to help.

It was a simple question, yet in those few seconds, I got all wound up and worried about how I'd be perceived. Dramas like that played out in my head all the time. I couldn't even sit in a doctor's office and pick up a magazine without wondering what others thought.

I'd sure like to look at that magazine with the three buxom swim-suit models, but that old lady would probably think I was a pervert. I guess I could look at People, *after all, I like the one-liner blurbs about the latest Hollywood smut, but that magazine is kind of trailer-trashy and I don't want anyone to think I'm low-brow. I wish I could read the* Popular Mechanics *over by that little girl, but if I tried to reach for it, her mom would probably think I was some kind of creeper trying to make a move on her daughter. I guess I'll just read Time; at least that one's safe.*

As I started paying more attention to this voice, I began to realize how often it was concerned with the opinions of others. It was like my intent was to always look good, which on the surface seems like a reasonable thing to do. I mean, why not go out there and make yourself look good? But if I was forgoing the things I wanted for the sake of my image, then who was in control of my life, me or my audience?

It was neither, really, it was the perception of my audience. It was the stories I was making up in my head. These other people didn't even have to say or do anything; my judgment took care of that. I'd size them up by how they dressed, by how they carried themselves, by what I thought of their education, and by a hundred other factors. I'd be standing in a food line deciding whether to grab a second cookie, and the decision might have come down to the person standing behind me. Was it an over-weight person, who I could assume would also grab another cookie, or the healthy type, who wouldn't? Most of the time my story was wrong, and I ended up wishing I'd just selected what-ever I originally wanted.

As I became aware of this dynamic, I began to understand the consequences of the decisions I'd been making. I had been telling myself for years that because I was a man, I should eat man-sized meals, so I ate man-sized burgers and always chose the largest steak on the menu. I also believed that a real man had a cast-iron stomach, able to digest whatever he was given, so I felt no need to watch my diet or read the labels on my groceries. Since I was tall, I thought my height-to-weight ratio should be that of a professional football player, so I settled on 240 pounds to match my 6-foot-4-inch height. And since that made me a big and tall man, I needed to wear extra-large shirts, because that's what lumberjacks with broad shoulders and barrel-sized chests wear as they rip branches off trees with their bare hands.

Never mind the fact that I didn't feel good when I weighed 240; I was lethargic, my face was fat, and my belly hung over my belt. So, I decided to trim down to a healthier weight. In pursuit of my weight loss, I learned from Fredi that a junior-size burger was all my body needed to sustain my weight. And I won't deny it; to this day, I still feel like a little girl when I order one. As for those extra-large shirts, I looked like a little boy wearing his dad's clothes. I don't have broad shoulders and my barrel sized chest more closely resembles a roll of paper towels. So, I started to wear large shirts instead and they fit me much better.

The problem was that I wanted to be something I wasn't. Somewhere along the way, I convinced myself that real men had certain attributes and I'd compare myself to that image to see how I sized up. Unfortunately, I only compared myself to the best. I compared my arms to those of the bodybuilders, my style and my looks to the leading actors of the world, and the size of my cock to porn stars with middle names like *The Python* or *The Shaft*. Speaking of which, of course I bought the extra-large condoms! What man wants to buy the regular size? Did it matter that if I turned around too fast, it would fly off?

What chance was there of me being happy if I was constantly comparing myself to the best? It was a no-win scenario; I would always be less than. And was it really the best I was comparing myself to, or just what society labels the best?

We love our extroverts and social types in America, but I'm not built like that. They have a way of making mundane things sound amusing, a skill I've never possessed. At times, I can't even make *interesting* things sound interesting. Social types possess a quick wit, and I don't have one. My comebacks are dry, poorly timed, and usually come out of my mouth all garbled. I don't even get jokes fast; I often start laughing after everyone else has already stopped.

Does any of that really matter? The social types are good at what they do, so why not let them have the spotlight? I'm not sure why I felt so driven to compete. I think it's because the social types always seem to attract a crowd of people no matter what they're doing. It's like they don't even have to try. I guess I just figured that they're so good at making people laugh, that they must be constantly having fun and getting laid.

I wanted to be like that... but I'm not.

When I pulled over a car for speeding and was invited by the three attractive ladies inside to party at their place after work, did I lower my sunglasses to get a better look at them before asking whether I should bring an extra pair of handcuffs? Of course not! I babbled something about slowing down and gracious invitation in the same sentence before walking back to my car all flustered.

It's not that I didn't want to party and have sex with three babes in a bubble-filled hot tub, I'm just not the guy who does that. Had I gone, we might have had a few drinks together, but in a failed attempt to make small talk, I would have convinced them that we needed to wash their cat. It's not that I don't enjoy being spontaneous and naughty and wild, I'm actually quite talented in that department, I'm just not comfortable being that way with strangers. This might explain why, in dating, my girl-friends often had to make the first move.

The world is filled with all kinds of people, and each of them possesses different skills, qualities, and attributes. There's no way I could have competed with them all. I, for one, will never have a savage tan; my milky white skin and bald head assure me of that. I can't even enjoy a Pina Colada on the beach without my skin beginning to smolder and smoke. I'll never be that guy who remembers your name at a party or thoughtfully sends you a card on your birthday; I can't even remember my wife or son's birthday and if you ask me their middle names, I'd have to stop and think about it.

The sad part is that I couldn't even appreciate these magnificent qualities in other people. If they remembered my name, I'd scold myself for not remembering theirs. If I saw them being great with their children, I'd berate myself for not being better with mine. How can I appreciate a fit person if I'm busy shaming myself for not being more fit? No wonder I had poor self-esteem; I was constantly reminding myself that I wasn't good enough.

It's okay I'm not good at everything. It's okay I'm absent-minded and my memory sucks. It's okay that I'm one of those guys who gets lost in my thoughts and stares blankly into space. Others have told me that they thought I was stupid when they first met me. I'm not stupid, I'm just theoretical and out of the box in my thinking. My mind is always looking for associations between different concepts, busily absorbing new information while cramming it into a giant spider web of thought and understanding.

Proudly show me your new sofa, and my mind will get to work determining how you angled it through your narrow entryway, what the manufacturer did to force the material to hug the concave curve on the back, and whether the armrests will get sun-bleached based on the positioning of your skylight.

While you might be waiting for me to say something like, "Oh, so pretty!", it's possible I'll be standing off to one side looking for footprints on the stairs. While this may lead you to believe I'm somewhat dim, what you don't know is that I've already established everything there is to know about your couch and am only looking for footprints because I'm attempting to answer the last remaining question that continues to elude me. And that is whether your three children use your brand-new sofa to springboard themselves from the stairs to the recliner across the room because, hell, that's what I would have done!

As I continued to become aware of who I was, several realizations occurred to me in rapid succession. First, I began to accept myself. No, it was more than that. I was beginning to love myself; me and all of my qualities. Coupled with that was the realization that if someone dislikes me or judges me for something I've said or done, then fine. Why try to control it? If they can't accept me, then why waste my time trying to change their mind? This was a significant discovery since I'd always tried so hard before to get people to like me.

Do you know those movies where the guy wants the girl, but the girl isn't interested, so the guy keeps trying until he wins her over? That was me, except by the time my song and dance was over, the girl still wasn't interested. Such was the case when I became enchanted with a woman in my Emergency Medical Technician (EMT) class. I asked her on a date, but she said no. The two of us seemed so compatible and had the greatest conversations, I just couldn't figure out why she wouldn't go out with me. It never occurred to me that I wasn't her type. These women I admired might have only liked guys with blue eyes, guys who liked country music, or guys who didn't catch fire while drinking Pina Colada's on the beach. I interpreted their refusal as something personal, something wrong with me, but it wasn't. As it turned out, the girl in my class was a lesbian; how in the hell was I going to win that one? The only thing her *no* meant was that she wasn't interested, and I just needed to move on.

The same thing happened while testing for promotion at work. After one such effort, I received written feedback from an interviewer who only mentioned my uniform and nothing else. He'd said my uniform wasn't tailored and that a loose string had been hanging from a seam on my shoulder.

"Who the fuck does he think he is?" I asked my partner, "I wore my best uniform that day and I even ironed it! Besides, what the hell does my uniform have to do with being a good supervisor?"

I blamed that reviewer for not getting the promotion and took it personal, but it wasn't. He simply thought a professional image topped the list of qualities needed by a police supervisor. It could have been anything. Maybe he was looking for a certain characteristic: someone more organized, a person who would crack down on non-performers, or maybe someone that he could fantasize about spanking in his dead mother's wedding dress. There could be a million reasons he might have chosen me, and it could have come down to whether I said good morning to him three months earlier when I saw him and his family at the mall. It made me realize that I just had to be myself, and either that's what he was looking for, or it wasn't.

I'd been taking these rejections as something personal. That somehow, I wasn't good enough, but it had nothing to do with me. We each have our own set of standards and criteria of what we like and what we don't, so why bother trying to change someone else's mind? It's kind of like trying to convince someone whose favorite fruit is apples that they should like oranges instead. Why bother? Take me, for instance. I'm a tall guy, but for whatever reason, I'm attracted to short women. I have no explanation for this. I have no reason. It doesn't even make sense. I just do. And much like I judge people for being fat, or from the South, or for wearing a crucifix, why shouldn't I think they aren't making similar judgments of me?

My *never-give-up* philosophy was causing a lot of anxiety and stress for nothing. I was fighting for all these people to choose me, and when they didn't, I'd just end up trying harder and harder. For some things in life, surrender is a better option.

This realization brought about another change in me as well. That little voice that I told you about, the one that was incessantly talking in my head asking whether I should or shouldn't work the late shift; it disappeared. I always thought the voice was coming from my mind and that it was giving me good advice, but it wasn't. The voice was just my insecurity, playing out various scenarios, busily flipping back and forth to calculate the most favorable outcome for me. Now when someone asks me a question, there is no voice; all that drama and tension is gone. I no longer get stuck thinking about what I should or shouldn't do; I just do what feels right.

As these changes occurred, a wonderful thing happened. Not only did I begin to appreciate myself and the person I'd become, but I began to appreciate others as well. There was no longer a competition going on with everyone I met. I could see the weaknesses of others, without feeling superior, and appreciate their strengths, without feeling inferior. No longer in competition with those around me, I had become free to connect with them instead.

I'm not sure I'd ever done that before, because somehow this connection felt different.

It felt good.

15

MEN ARE PUSSIES

"Can we talk about what happened tonight?" asked every woman I ever dated.

I dreaded this question. For whatever reason, my girlfriend at the time always wanted to discuss the argument on the same night it happened, usually when I was tired and climbing into bed. From experience, the ensuing conversation would last for hours.

I never understood why women wanted to talk about arguments; couldn't they just sleep on it and let things get better in the morning?

"Ok... we can talk."

What happened next was a mystery to me. She would say something like, "When you looked at that woman with big boobs, I got scared you'd leave me and began to cry."

My reply to such statements was typically something like, "Oh for god's sake, I just glanced at her!"

My girlfriend would then enter into a strange ritual where she would keep rehashing the events of the evening while I did my best to stay awake. At some point, unable to keep from nodding off, I'd apologize for my actions, even if I didn't think that I'd done anything wrong. I found this to be the only way to get her to stop talking so that I could finally get some sleep.

It wasn't until I met Fredi that I began to understand the dynamics underlying these discussions. The problem was that my girlfriend assumed she was speaking with an emotionally mature adult, but she wasn't. I didn't understand the language of emotions because that part of my brain had stopped developing when I was still a kid.

So, when my girlfriend said, "When you looked at the woman with big boobs, I got scared you'd leave me and began to cry." I never received her message. I didn't realize she was being vulnerable and sharing her fears with me. I didn't know that all she was asking for was a hug and some reassurance that I still loved her.

Instead, what I heard was, "When you looked at that woman with big boobs, it made me cry." The message I received was an accusation. I translated her words to mean that I was eyeballing this other woman like a heartless bastard and this is what made her cry. That's why I felt compelled to defend myself by saying, "Oh for god's sake, I just glanced at her!"

I also didn't realize that I had been the one driving the mysterious ritual of rehashing the incident. I believe this is because my girlfriend, upon seeing I hadn't received her message, was trying to clarify herself by redescribing the event in different terms. However, her rehashing just sounded like more accusations, which served only to numb my brain and lead me to think, *Yeah, yeah, yeah, I got it. I'm a heartless bastard. Can we go to sleep now?*

Believing there would be no end to the conversation, I typically offered my apology in hopes of a speedier resolution. Interestingly, while I concluded that my apology was what had ended these discussions, I don't think it was. Unaware my girlfriend wasn't looking for an apology, I believe what brought her comfort was the various "I love you" statements that came along with my apology. I'm not sure my girlfriend ever felt like the argument was fully resolved, nor understood why I was apologizing, but I think she heard that I still loved her and felt that at least some progress had been made.

While an apology is not what she wanted, I'd been living under the presumption that all post-argument discussions required one. In my mind, the purpose of these discussions was to assert fault so that the guilty party could apologize. In this case, either I had to apologize for making her cry, or she had to apologize for overreacting to my glance.

However, on those occasions when I was too angry to apologize, I'd resort to what my father taught me: stuff my emotions and don't let the incident bother me. I would emotionally disconnect and give my girlfriend the silent treatment. I often stayed like this for days or even weeks, usually until I forgot the details of the argument or was distracted by something else. And that something else was typically the makeup sex that followed these catastrophic discussions. *Ahh, that's better... argument is officially over.*

At the time, I felt good about how I handled these talks. I assumed that since I wasn't yelling or acting aggressively, I was demonstrating my ability to control my emotions and was therefore a man with whom a woman could feel safe. However, as I look back at it now, I understand how wrong I was. They may have felt physically safe, but I was emotionally abandoning them at a time when they most needed connection, and I'm guessing that didn't feel safe at all.

Fredi has since helped me develop my emotional self; I'm now somewhere in the 7th grade. While my tendency is still to withdraw during these discussions, she'll often help me understand the dynamics of what's happening by talking me through it. Sometimes, that's as simple as telling me she needs a hug. I need her to say it like that because human touch is counterintu- itive to me. That's because my habit during these discussions is not to be open, vulnerable, or to seek understanding, but to prepare for battle.

Fredi and I talked about my need to battle, and she suggested that I do this because I've already decided why the argument happened. She explained it like this: *When a person asks us, "Can we talk about it", and we're not in a place where we are willing to hear a different viewpoint, then that question implies our viewpoint is wrong. So, rather than listening and being open to what the other person is saying, we feel compelled to explain why our view- point is right.*

Her explanation had merit, after all, my post-argument discussions usually did resemble a trial. In the case of me looking at the woman with big boobs, my defense against my girlfriends' accusations would have typically employed one of the following strategies:

- Ignorance/Denial: "Who are you talking about? What woman with big boobs?"
- Justification: "Honey, everyone was looking at her boobs!"
- Mitigation: "Big, yes, but much too saggy... I prefer yours."
- Counterclaim: "Me? You were the one flirting with Mr. Tight Pants at the bar!"
- Extenuating circumstance: "It's true, I was looking at her; I was captivated by her pendant."
- Minimizing: "Honey, don't you think you're kind of over-reacting?"

In this case, I felt compelled to defend myself because I'd already determined why my girlfriend was upset. She was angry at me because I'd been ogling this other woman like a heartless bastard. However, what I failed to notice was that my girlfriend never claimed to be angry, nor did she accuse me of being a heartless bastard. That was my doing.

I was calling myself a heartless bastard because I knew the truth. I wasn't just looking at this other woman's boobs, I was already nestled between them, basking in the warmth of her bosom like a curled-up little kitten.

My girlfriend didn't catch me looking, she caught me fantasizing. She had every right to be mad. I was frolicking about the land of monstrous mammaries like a horny little elf. However, I was so busy shaming myself for getting caught that I couldn't hear what she said. She wasn't angry at me. She knew why I was looking, and probably knew what I was thinking, but all she wanted to know was that I still loved her.

As I learned to pay more attention to these conversations, I realized just how often I hadn't been listening. Instead, I had been filtering these conversations through the lenses of my own beliefs. I was so busy listening to the narrative in the back of my mind, that I couldn't hear what others were trying to tell me. I trusted my judgment, more than I trusted their words.

That's what happened with my high school girlfriend when she went to Spain. I wasn't reading her letters and listening to what she was saying; I was listening to the stories I made up in my head. I was injecting my own facts about her drinking binges, dirty dancing, and wild romances with Spanish men. I didn't trust that she loved me because I trusted my stories more than her.

It's also what happened when I found Oscar the Grouch in the toy bin. I intended to take Oscar home to sleep with, but when the kid from school approached, I made up a story that he'd call me a baby for sleeping with a stuffed animal. So, I told him I planned to feed Oscar to my dog. But what if I hadn't?

What if I'd told him the truth? Instead of saying, "cool!", would he have turned to his mom and asked for his own Oscar to sleep with? Would the two of us stood in line, hugging our Oscars, only to become closer friends as a result?

The stories I made up in my head were costing me opportunities to connect. That's what happened in SWAT when I was afraid to admit I got tunnel vision. I thought everyone would laugh, but when our breacher admitted his nervousness that led him to smash down the door, all it did was bring the team closer together. It could have been me that made that happen, but because I was scared to admit my tunnel vision, the credit went to him.

I think back to the conversations my family used to have around the dinner table and I realize how bland they were. Our discussions were filled with superficial bullshit. We'd talk about the weather and politics, and whenever someone asked how someone else was doing, the answer was invariably, "Fine, fine, everything's fine". The only time we talked about ourselves was when we announced some kind of triumph or described how someone had slighted us. The conversations had no depth; even our hugs were shallow and fake.

I think this is the consequence of being raised in a judgmental household. Our father's never-ending criticism made it unsafe to speak the truth. We all knew that we had to be strong and tough because anything else was ridiculous. So, we could either brag, complain about someone else, or talk about the weather, none of which are topics that provide compelling reasons to connect with others.

Meanwhile, dinner with Fredi's family comes with an entirely different vibe. Warm hugs are the norm, and conversations have a depth that is difficult to describe. When Fredi's brother had his birthday, one of his sisters began asking him his birthday questions. Questions like, "What were you most proud

of this year?" and, "What was the biggest challenge you faced?"
He had just finished building a house for his family and spoke
of the difficulties he experienced while positioning the 50 ft
main beam of the house by himself and the anguish he experienced when an unexpected storm struck and filled his basement
with 8 feet of snow before the roof had been installed. He told us
of the complicated building codes he worked through, the
helpful inspector who gave him pointers, and the challenge of
living with his family in an RV for over a year. In the end, he
concluded that building his home was both his biggest challenge and his proudest achievement.

He wasn't boasting, nor asking for pity, he was just
describing the experience of building a home by himself and
the different ways it had affected him and his family. In return,
there was no judgment of what he said, only understanding.
There's a depth that comes with a conversation that is so open
and honest, a depth that others can sense. We can all tell when
someone is being authentic, and I believe that this is the key to
human connection.

If I wanted to build that level of trust and connection with
others, I'd have to start telling the truth. At the risk of getting
laughed at or scorned, I'd have to open up and share how I truly
felt. To build trust, I'd have to show trust, and that would be
risky. I would have to expose myself to the possibility of being
hurt, embarrassed, or made fun of, and that would require me to
be vulnerable.

But to allow myself to be vulnerable would not be easy.
Vulnerability was not something my winning set of philosophies
allowed. They dictated that to be tough I had to remain strong
and not let anything bother me. And this was a problem because
vulnerable was not a word I associated with strength. Vulnerable
was a word used to describe a bunny hiding in a hole. Vulnerable was a child who cried because his feelings got hurt. Vulner-

able was not a SWAT guy leading his team into danger; but the guy who shrieks when approached by a spider. Vulnerable was the word I used to describe pussies and victims and weak people who couldn't defend themselves, and that wasn't me.

I was invulnerable.

I was the guy who wasn't bothered by little things. If someone said mean things to me, I just let it ricochet off my armor. I was tough and tough guys don't do vulnerable.

But here's the interesting thing; it's not the emotional guys that are pussies, it's the invulnerable guys like me. That's because guys like me aren't invulnerable, we just pretend we are. We get our feelings hurt, just like everyone else, but have spent a lifetime hiding and stuffing our emotions. We're the ones who learned not to cry so that we wouldn't be made fun of at school. We're the ones who act passive-aggressively to hide what we're really feeling inside. We do these things because we're scared of letting others know the truth, the truth that we too can be hurt.

Brenee Brown, a well-known shame researcher, relates the topic of vulnerability to soldiers. She says that the soldiers who win medals for bravery are the ones who place themselves at risk to accomplish their mission, not the ones who hide behind their armor and play it safe. Placing yourself in a vulnerable position takes courage. The brave ones in a relationship are those who admit their feelings to connect with others, not the guys like me who talk about our accomplishments, bitch about other people, and provide periodic updates on the weather.

When my girlfriend told me she was scared, she made herself vulnerable. It took bravery to do that. She opened herself up to a range of responses that might have been painful. Had I laughed or made fun of her, thus violating her trust, she would have used her boundaries to protect herself and send me back to the singles market.

I didn't realize I could protect myself with boundaries,

because I was still a kid when my dad taught me to stop crying and stuff my emotions. I hadn't learned that I didn't have to take another person's actions or responses to heart because I was still at that emotional age when I was blaming others for how they made me feel. I didn't realize I had a choice

Unfortunately, since I didn't want my girlfriends blaming me for making them feel bad, I felt compelled to caretake their feelings instead. I didn't think they were strong enough to hear the truth, so I'd often tell them what I thought they wanted to hear instead.

I wasn't comforting them; I was bullshitting them.

A few months ago, I was getting ready for work when Fredi came out of the bedroom staring groggily at her phone. I was happy to see her. I was glad we could spend a few minutes together before I left because, normally, she's still asleep. As she sat on the couch across from me, I could hear that she was watching a video on how to make a porcelain elf. Not wanting to interrupt her, I waited for the video to end so that we could talk. However, after it ended, she never looked up. Instead, she switched over to her news feed where she looked through several articles before stopping to read out loud a headline regarding something the President had said. Expecting her to glance up to see my reaction, I watched as she clicked over to Facebook to begin scrolling through her friend's latest posts. With only a minute left before I needed to leave, the veins in my forehead began pulsing.

Fredi knew better than this. She knew that her behavior was rude. We often spoke of the disconnection we saw in other couples who go to restaurants and stare at their phones without talking. In addition, she'd also been very strict with my son's phone usage, and often told me about having to teach her patients good phone boundaries as well. Oh yes, she knew better than this, and worse yet, this was not the first time. She'd been doing a lot of this lately and my resentment was starting to grow.

Now, the old me would have considered opening the door and throwing her phone in the snow. The old me wouldn't have actually done that but certainly would have imagined it. The new me also wanted to throw her phone in the snow but decided it would be better to say something first. I considered asking, "Do you think you can survive for five minutes without your goddamn phone?" However, I knew this sounded a little too aggressive and over the top, so I paused for a minute to think it over. I had to reframe my words in order to sound like an emotionally mature adult. I had to tell her how I was feeling. Well, I felt like she was having an affair with her phone, but accusing her of having an affair didn't seem all that wise either. I had to make it sound like I trusted her and like it wasn't her fault. I had to use tact...

"If your phone was a dude, I'd punch him in the face!", I snarled.

I'll confess... this wasn't one of my finer moments.

Looking up from her phone, she chuckled and said, "What?"

"Your phone! You keep looking at your damn phone! I've got like one minute before I have to leave and all you can do is stare at your goddamn phone! Can't we just talk?"

"Honey, you don't have to get so upset, just ask for what you need."

Did she just tell me that I should ask for what I need? I don't need anything! Need is for losers who can't take care of themselves. This wasn't my problem; this was hers! She's the one that made me angry. She's the one being rude. Why in the hell should I be the one to get on my knees and beg for what I need? I'll show her what I need...

"Whatever", I mumbled as I stormed out the front door, slamming it closed behind me.

On my way to work, I replayed the argument in my head. I'd blamed her for pissing me off, but I knew better than that. I needed to look deeper. I needed to find the source of my anger. The story I made up was that she knew better, and therefore she was being rude, but was that fair, or was I just trying to shame her because she *should* have known that I wanted to talk?

Fredi would later describe my reaction like this: *There is an element of victimhood when someone isn't treating us the way we think they should. We don't know what's going on for them, which is why it's so important to ask for what we need. However, even if we ask, they still get to choose whether they comply. If we are properly taking care of our needs, their response doesn't matter, because emotionally healthy adults don't need anyone to do anything for them; it just feels nice when they do. For example, sometimes I want a hug because it would help tremendously - it's not that I need one, I just want one. If you decide to give me a hug, great, if not, then it's up to me to find another way to comfort myself. Healthy relationships include an interdependence where there is a mix of give and take, but ultimately, we're responsible for meeting our own needs.*

She was right. I'd been playing the role of the victim. I blamed her for making me mad because I made up the story that her phone was more important than me.

I used to do the same thing to her when she would get a snack during a movie without asking me if I wanted one too. My love language is acts of service, and so when I get up during a movie, I always ask if she wants something too. So, when she'd get up without asking, I'd wait until she sat back down before blasting her for not offering to get me something. It's like, rather than being vulnerable by admitting I needed something, I would set a trap so that I could be the victim, and then shame her for not being more thoughtful.

Instead of blaming her for not putting down the phone, I should have said something like, "Honey, would you mind if we spend a few minutes talking before I leave for work?" This most certainly would have been a better approach because, had she said no, then I could have thrown her phone in the snow... although, I suppose that wouldn't have demonstrated very good boundaries.

I'm not sure why she puts up with me.

PART III

A CLOSER LOOK

16

JUDGMENT DAY

A few years ago, Fredi's brother hosted a dining event in tribute to the French cookbook author, Julia Child. He purchased the ingredients for several recipes along with a half dozen bottles of wine before inviting his siblings and their spouses over to spend the evening preparing and devouring what turned out to be a magnificent feast. Since all of us enjoy cooking fresh foods and drinking fine wines, that evening marked the first of many themed events to follow.

On this particular night, we had gathered for Greek Fest, and curious for some feedback, I had just finished reading out loud my chapter titled, *THE APPLE THAT DIDN'T FALL FAR FROM THE CHRISTMAS TREE.* The image of my son pushing that giant Christmas tree box up the stairs, contrasted with me sitting in my recliner, makes me laugh to this day. I'm not sure why I find that moment so funny; I think the story just illustrates me as such a horrible dad that I can't believe I'm willing to share it with the world.

So, when I looked up after finishing the chapter and saw everyone was in tears, their response didn't correlate with my expectations. They weren't supposed to be crying; they were supposed to be reprimanding me.

Unsure of how to respond, I turned to Fredi for assistance.

"Why are they crying?" I whispered.

"Because they liked your story."

"But why are they sobbing?"

"Because they connected with what you said."

Her explanation didn't make sense. I'm an unemotional guy; how could I write something that would elicit such an emotional response? Confused, and more than a bit curious, I turned to her brother and asked him to explain. He told me that my story caused him to weep because it led him to think about his son and all the times he failed as a parent himself. Fredi's sisters then echoed a similar sentiment, describing how each of them had reminisced on their parenting mishaps as well.

It took me a few days to comprehend what happened that night. Her siblings had shown me empathy and grace. By relating my imperfections to their own, they were able to connect and show me support and understanding. Rather than heaping shame on me by declaring "you suck", their message had been more akin to "what you did sucked, but we understand how you feel, because we've done sucky things like that ourselves".

This may have been the first time I comprehended the meaning of empathy. I always considered myself to be an empathetic person but hadn't realized empathy requires connection. What I previously considered to be empathy was a conscious thought process devoid of emotion and shared experience. For example, when interviewing a victim of rape, my interpretation of empathy had been the learned response that the victim had been traumatized, and therefore I should show compassion by talking softly and not subjecting this person to physical contact. While I could intellectually understand how a forced assault may have left this person feeling powerless and vulnerable, I wasn't capable of connection. Instead, I had been using an analytical thought process to determine their feelings and the most appropriate response.

While writing this book, I asked several friends and family members to review my various drafts. The feedback I received from those with the capacity to empathize said it was a page-turner and praised me for showing such vulnerability. However, the feedback I received from self-declared unemotional types was that the book painted me as an unlikeable fellow, and while I had shared several personal ah-ha moments, they couldn't see why anyone else would be interested in reading it.

These comments disappointed me because I had specifically written this book for unemotional types like me. I wanted to share with them the lessons I'd learned. I thought these concepts seemed so universal, yet once I wrote them down, they seemed to have no impact on these guys at all. But why?

My first thought was that these unemotional types didn't like my book because they read it without emotions. They read about an unfaithful husband, a disconnected father, a self-serving boyfriend, an insecure team leader, and an overall angry and manipulative man. Reading my story without emotions, they were only able to understand half my book. They couldn't feel the hurt and abandonment I experienced from my father. They couldn't experience my insecurity, my fears, or the depth of my worthlessness. And if you can't experience those feelings, how can you understand the desperation I felt to find a perfect woman so that the other guys would admire me? How can you make sense of how badly I craved the respect of my SWAT team? My actions aren't justifiable if you can't connect with my emotions.

However, there was a flaw in my theory. While reviewing my book, one of these unemotional guys had written a summary after each chapter, and his summaries accurately captured my feelings and dysfunctions. Even without an emotional connection, they still understood my story.

I didn't know what to think. Maybe they were right. I mean, admittedly, my dysfunctions did seem rather obvious once I discovered them, so why should I think anyone else would find them insightful? And it wasn't like I disagreed with their assessment, after all, wasn't I the one who expected Fredi's family to reprimand me for the way I'd raised my son? If I was unable to accept the things I'd done, then how could I expect them to?

I dwelled on these questions for almost a year. The problem was that the lessons I learned from Fredi dramatically changed my life. They were so impactful, that they motivated me to write this book. While admittedly, we all have our dysfunctions, wouldn't at least one or two of my chapters resonate with these guys?

I turned to Fredi for perspective.

"Well, how would you describe the guys who read your book?", she asked.

"Umm... unemotional, judgmental, perfectionistic?"

"OK, so now think about what you wrote. Your book is all about your imperfections and vulnerabilities, both of which are seen as negative qualities by perfectionistic people. In essence, you've given them a whole book of reasons by which to judge you, so why are you surprised they don't like it?"

"Because..., well..., I thought I could show them how all these lessons I learned had changed my life. I was so careful to describe how I'd been judging myself and all these other people so harshly, and how once I'd learned to question my stories, my life and relationships suddenly improved."

"That's true, but here's the problem. Judgmental people tend to judge themselves harder than they judge other people. That's because they have a low tolerance for imperfections and vulner-

abilities, both in themselves and others. They have a low tolerance because they have high expectations, so high that they
often find it difficult to accept their own imperfections and
vulnerabilities. That's why you often see perfectionistic people
flogging themselves endlessly whenever they screw something
up. Rather than accepting their humanity when making
mistakes, they heap shame on themselves instead. And that is at
the core of the problem, because if you can't accept your imperfections and vulnerabilities, how can you accept them in
someone else? This dynamic is what gave rise to the expression
that you can't love other people until you first love yourself. Or,
as my sister is fond of saying, you first have to accept the jackass
in the mirror before you can accept the one standing next to
you."

Everything she said fit with what I'd experienced. The judgment, the shame, the resulting love I felt for myself, the sudden
connection I felt to others, it was all there. Her description even
explained why the unemotional types didn't like my book.
However, even if they were judging me harshly, wouldn't they at
least connect with some of the things I said? Once again, I
turned to Fredi.

"People sometimes need to hear the same thing a hundred
different times before they connect the dots and get it. I've had
patients tell me that they were enlightened by something they
just heard when it was the same something I'd been pointing
out to them for years. The words just have to be in the right
context and come at the right time for the person to hear them."

"But honey", she continued, "a word of caution. You can't
write your book expecting others to be enlightened by what you
wrote. We are each self-aware in different ways, and it is
because of these differences that we each need to follow our
own path. Don't get me wrong, your book is important, and I
have no doubt that some will find it impactful and possibly

even life-changing, but don't expect that kind of reaction from everyone."

She was right. I had been wanting to be affirmed by my unemotional readers. I wanted them to say that my book had kicked their dysfunctional ass. My ego was getting in the way. I had to stop thinking about impressing my readers and get back to writing my story.

So, I stopped thinking about these guys and started reflecting on what Fredi said. I was intrigued by her comments regarding judgmental people, and how their high standards drive them to be hard on themselves. Those words resonated with me. I wondered whether this dynamic might help me answer the one question that still plagued me:

If my dysfunctions were so obvious, then why hadn't I noticed them before?

17

THE SAINT

The lectures in philosophy class had chipped away at the faith of my classmate, leading her to question the existence of God. During one of these lectures, she blurted out, "You mean, I did all that volunteer work for nothing?"

My jaw dropped. The ramifications of her statement silenced the class. She hadn't been volunteering at the homeless shelter because she cared for other people, she'd been volunteering to earn her ticket to heaven. The only person she'd been trying to help was herself!

I ran my first marathon when I was 44. I wasn't a runner, nor did I enjoy running, I just wanted to prove I could go the distance without stopping; that's what strong runners do. Aware this would not be easy, I shared my intentions with everyone I knew, that way my pride would keep me from backing out. I spent that summer running at least three times per week, following the minimum training guidelines, and by the day of the race, I was ready to go.

It was still dark when I arrived at the starting location, but within minutes, the morning sun painted the clouds with a pallet of pink and orange hues. The air was cool and crisp and the forecast predicted clear skies and mild temperatures; it was turning out to be a magnificent day. The runners had already gathered near the starting line, so I wormed my way into the middle of the crowd. I had no expectations of winning this event or even leading my age group; I just wanted to finish strong.

When the starting gun fired, it took a few seconds for the inertia of this large group of runners to get moving, but once they did, it was like a levee broke as we all streamed out onto the trail. Giddy with excitement, my body felt half its weight as I floated along the path, carried by the current of a thousand other runners. However, this sensation abruptly vanished when a pea-sized rock landed inside my shoe. The opening stretch of the race was on a gravel path that bordered a lake, and the sudden onslaught of closely spaced runners created a frenzy of pea-sized bouncing rocks. As I passed several contestants who'd stopped to empty their shoes, I discovered I could minimize the discomfort of the stone by controlling its placement with my toes.

I promised myself I wouldn't stop and I meant it. Winners never quit.

By the third or fourth mile, the runners had stretched out along the path as each fell into their natural rhythms. Looking around, I took note of those closest to me: a few were older, one had a limp, and based on the breathing of the guy behind me, I wasn't sure he'd survive the race. Confident I could do better than this group, I gradually increased my speed.

Moving ahead, I fell in with another band of runners who appeared to be fit and closer to my age. I was content at that pace for several miles until I spotted a younger woman with long dark hair running ahead. It was her bottom that caught my attention; I couldn't look away. Extending past the width of her shoulders, her rear end had stretched her spandex shorts into a state of semi-transparency. Hers was not the lean buttocks of a marathon runner, but of one who watches too much TV. Unable to comprehend how she'd managed to outpace me, I once again increased my speed, eventually passing her near the midpoint of the course. I was now running faster than I had in practice.

Every few miles, rest areas provided free water and snacks to runners. I carried my own supply of refreshments and discovered these pit stops served as the ideal location to overtake those more difficult-to-pass runners as they stopped to refresh themselves. However, near mile 18, I took a sip from my hydration pack and was met with the unwelcome gurgle that signaled my water supply had run out. Already thirsty, and with eight miles yet to go, I knew I'd be forced to rely on the remaining aid stations for hydration.

The perspiration flowing from under my hat kept saturating my eyebrows, periodically releasing a torrent of sweat that stung and blurred my vision. To conserve my dwindling supply of body fluids, I reduced my speed, and in far less time than anticipated was passed by the woman with the large buttocks. Flustered, I sped up, but was unable to maintain her pace for long and was thereafter left to watch as her rear end disappeared into the horizon like a ship bobbing out to sea. Ashamed at first, I decided not to let it bother me, after all, I should have brought more water.

No longer able to counteract the effects of dehydration, my stride degraded into a lumbering run. With my ever-slowing pace, the time to run between mile markers increased, creating the illusion that the distance between markers had also increased. On more than one occasion, I was so certain I'd run two miles, when the mile marker reflected only one, that I began to suspect I'd fallen victim to a careless race official who'd improperly marked the course.

The persistent sunshine had burned away the crisp morning air and now seemed determined to thwart my body's ability to cool itself. My mouth hung open from panting; my tongue felt coated in flour. Concerned with how much long I could last, I cursed the organizers for not adding more pit stops near the end. However, my fear of dehydration was quenched when I spotted a table of refreshments in a grass field ahead. Maintaining my loping gait, I slowed enough to grab two cups of water from the volunteers manning the station. Holding my arms outstretched to absorb the shock of my run, I attempted to drink from each cup in succession, spilling far more water onto my shirt than what poured into my mouth. I briefly considered running in a circle to grab two more cups, but quickly struck the thought from my mind; turning around would have felt too much like stopping and there was no way I would consider that.

Dehydrated, overheated, and now disheartened, I continued my run. The contenders who passed me now were those I'd seen much earlier. These were the men and women with questionable hips and knees, and those who'd been born decades before me. Summoning my will to continue, I paced myself against these stragglers while reaffirming my vow to never give up.

As the pathway curved into the entrance of a public park, my muscles tensed at the sight of the checkered banner hanging less than 100 yards away. Having concluded this race would never end, the sudden onset of the finish line jolted me into an unexpected but most welcome new reality. Elated, I ran toward my well-deserved finish on a trajectory that took me off the sidewalk and into the grass. A volunteer, holding his hand out like a crossing guard, kindly informed me that I first had to circle the park's perimeter before crossing the finish line. Unaware he had just added a half mile or so to my much anticipated finish, and perhaps expecting to be thanked for his thoughtful assistance, he leapt back in surprise as I furrowed my brow and shouted, "Are you fucking kidding me!"

Grudgingly, I returned to the sidewalk to begin my trip around the park. The build-up of lactic acid was causing my leg muscles to seize, dramatically changing my form. I no longer resembled a marathon runner but a hunched over elderly man chasing a windswept piece of paper through a neighborhood parking lot. In the distance, I glimpsed my son emerge from a crowd of spectators to join me for the final stretch home. Excited and running at first, his expression morphed into concern as he transitioned into an awkward side-stepping walk to accommodate my slower speed. I would have preferred he stayed home that day; he should have been racing to keep up with his dad, not pausing to slow down.

Too parched to talk, and too weak to acknowledge my sons' efforts to motivate me, my eyes fixated on an empty folding chair standing just past the finish line. As I crossed the rubber timing mat, with that damn rock still in my shoe, I fell forward into the chair with enough momentum that it toppled over and collapsed while throwing me headlong into the grass. Content to lay as I'd landed, my nostrils sucked in fresh air through the dirt as my body took the opportunity to offload its heat into the cool earth below. Had the paramedics not come to rehydrate me, I would have gladly remained there till morning.

I'd done it. I'd completed my first marathon and had done so without stopping.

However, this wasn't the finish I'd envisioned. I'd not only placed in the bottom 46th percentile of all runners, but according to the small graphic shown on the race map, the elevation had gradually declined a total of 1,200 feet over the length of the course. How could I derive a sense of accomplishment from running a downhill marathon?

Winners never quit.

One year later, I completed my second and final marathon. Considered to be among the most difficult in the US, the Pikes Peak Marathon requires participants to run 13.1 miles up steep and rutted dirt trails to the summit of Pikes Peak (elevation 14,115 ft) before turning around to run back down. This time, I didn't fall across the finish line, I sprinted across.

Nobody could call me a loser now.

Which is an interesting conclusion for me to reach since nobody called me a loser before.

This tendency to judge ourselves based entirely on the story we make up in our minds is what makes judgment such an interesting topic. A runner might place first in a marathon and call himself a loser for not breaking the all-time course record, while another might place dead last and call himself a winner because, last year, he could barely climb a flight of stairs.

On the day of my first marathon, I could have chosen to embrace a variety of different stories. I might have congratulated myself for finishing something only one percent of the population has ever attempted. And even though my completion time placed me in the bottom 46th percentile, I could have concluded I'd done quite well for a first-time marathoner, especially for one who doesn't like to run. Rather than assuming the woman with the large buttocks spent her days watching TV, I might have wondered whether she was last year's champion but had grown a size or two after having a baby. Finally, was it really a downhill marathon? A 1,200-foot drop over 26.2 miles equates to one step down for every 114 steps taken, which isn't exactly the same as running down a hill.

However, I'm guessing I didn't tell myself those stories because they sounded too much like excuses, and winners never make excuses. Instead, they just keep pushing themselves harder and harder, which is why I ran my second marathon. I had to redeem myself.

But why?

The only thing I set out to do was run a marathon without stopping, and that's what I did. So, why wasn't that enough?

Fredi proposed the following: *People don't like being confronted with something that challenges their self-image; it feels threatening and uncomfortable. They may have spent decades developing a picture of who they are, and it's difficult to accept they aren't who they thought they were. So, rather than looking within to reassess their identity, they might feel ashamed for failing to live up to their idyllic self-image or perhaps seek to blame those uncomfortable feelings on someone else.*

That made sense. When the woman with the large buttocks passed me, I felt ashamed because her body shape challenged my self-image of being a strong runner. Likewise, when I yelled at that volunteer for telling me to run around the park, I was blaming him for exposing my lack of fortitude because by then, I was so exhausted I wasn't sure I could make it around the park.

But here's the interesting thing. Athletes generally take care of their needs. They monitor their performance and when they begin to wear down, they'll eat, drink, or do whatever else is necessary to get back in the game. Their focus is on finishing the race in the best time possible and not on trying to prove how much dehydration they can withstand.

Had I taken the time to stop, I could have rehydrated and finished my race much sooner, but instead, I kept running. I ran until my sweat ran dry and my muscles seized. I ran until I was so exhausted that I collapsed across the finish line.

I wasn't behaving like a strong runner but like someone who believed that *not stopping* was a matter of life or death. My actions weren't about me *wanting* to prove my resilience, they were about me *needing* to prove it.

I needed to prove that dehydration couldn't stop me. I needed to prove that I was tough, that I could push myself hard, that I had grit. I needed to prove that no matter how bad things got, I wouldn't quit, because that's what winners do.

Needing to prove myself is why I jumped from the highest cliff when cliff diving with friends, why I was the last one to board the scuba boat when it was surrounded by sharks, and why I felt compelled to chase a bear deep into the woods late at night. Needing to prove myself is why I was the only one to get fully tased in my TASER class, the last one to flee the gas chamber in my tear gas class, and the only one to be pepper sprayed with my eyes physically held open in my pepper spray class.

I needed to prove that I was tough and unafraid, because tough and unafraid is what made me better than other men. These were the qualities that gave me worth, and therefore the qualities for which I was most proud.

Unfortunately, the type of pride I was feeling was not the healthy type you get from learning to ride a bike, but the dysfunctional type you get from trying to convince yourself you're better than other people. They call this type of pride, false pride, because no matter how many times you prove it, it's never enough.

I was afraid to stop because stopping meant I wasn't a strong runner. It meant I wasn't worthy. It meant I was the loser I'd been trying so hard not to be.

I thought I'd overcome my insecurity years ago by adopting my winning set of philosophies, but I hadn't. Instead, no matter how well I did, my poor self-esteem would just find more reasons why I still wasn't good enough. I kept raising my bar of performance higher and higher until I could no longer reach it.

I look at my winning philosophies now and it's obvious why this occurred:

- Life is tough – you've got to fight for what you want

- The secret to success is never giving up
- You must stay strong and not let things bother you

Fight, never give up, and ignore your pain! These words weren't helping me overcome my insecurities, they were just helping me push them back with false pride.

Instead of using my discomfort as a signal to stop and drink, I'd been using it as proof of my grit. The more exhausted and crippled I became, the tougher I was proving myself to be, and therefore the more false pride I could claim.

A confident and secure person doesn't need to prove himself, nor does he need to be perfect, because he knows he's good enough just the way he is.

When I thought about this concept of false pride, I looked through my previous chapters and noticed a pattern begin to emerge. I discovered that I wasn't the dysfunctional guy you've been reading about, but someone else.

I was Mr. Honorable who stuck by his wedding vows. I was Mr. Righteous who didn't bend to corruption. I was Mr. Giving who donated money to sick children and Mr. Loving who promised commitment to every girlfriend. I was Mr. Responsible who covered the extra shift, Mr. Nice Guy who treated strangers with kindness, and Mr. Good Neighbor who would have kept quite if your dog peed on his rosebush.

I wasn't a dysfunctional man; I was a goddamn saint! I was the martyr of false pride.

My entire life had been built on a foundation of false pride. I was using my misery to prove what a wonderful person I was. I thought I was a good man who loved and honored his wife, but that was just the story I told myself. I resented her, but was using that resentment as proof of my chivalry and honor. I was miserable during that time but claimed I was proud because *a lesser man would have selfishly chosen to divorce her.* And the more miserable I became, the more proud I claimed to be.

This is why I couldn't see my dysfunctions. I was using my misery, not as a signal to change, but as proof of my goodness and grit. I had to keep running because without the pain, how could I show how tough I was? Without pain, how could I show how devoted I was to my wife, or how loyal I was to my work. My pain was the proof that made me great.

My mother made me a special soup and told me how much she hoped I would enjoy it. It was awful, but of course I told her I loved it. Every special occasion thereafter, she prepared her special soup for me. I faithfully choked it down for years while priding myself on what a loving son I was proving myself to be.

I did the same thing with gifts. Someone would give me a gift that I loathed, and I'd tell them how perfect it was. Then, fearing to throw it away in case they asked about it later, I'd end up placing it prominently on my mantle in case they came over to visit.

And there I was, telling myself what an honorable, grateful, and kind person I was, while sitting next to my crappy wife, sipping my mother's crappy soup, and staring at all the crappy presents hung on the wall.

I was claiming to be kindhearted and good but I was inauthentic, angry, and resentful. I'd created this weird association where the more anger and anguish I felt, the better person I was proving myself to be. It was a process that worked like this:

- The more I did what I should (*a dedicated worker should work the extra shift*),
- the more I let my boundaries slip (*agreeing to work when I didn't want to*),
- the more angry and resentful I became (*my boss is*

such a jackass for always asking me to work the extra shift),

- the more false pride I earned (I'm such a good employee; I stepped up to help while all those other selfish bastards went home*).*

I was telling myself that it's tough to be a good man, that I was one of the few who had the grit to do the right thing, but that was all a story. Being a good person only seemed tough because pain was the benchmark by which I measured the goodness of a person.

False pride is the carrot at the end of the stick. It compels its victims to constantly prove themselves, but no matter how often they do, it's never enough, because worthlessness can't be fixed with false pride.

I understand now why so many successful people might be unhappy and unfulfilled in their lives. False pride preys on success. It embeds itself in what feels like achievement. It strikes at the heart of famous comedians, brilliant astrophysicists, and highly paid athletes who know they're good, just not good enough.

I never thought to look for dysfunction in my grit because I constantly proved I had grit. And that's why false pride is so devious because, it's not that I wasn't tough or brave, it's that due to poor self-esteem, I could never be tough or brave enough.

The rich man knows he's rich, getting high with each million he makes, but no matter how big his pile of money becomes, it will never be enough. And that's why he ruthlessly cuts his employee's benefits because, yachts are expensive and he needs a new one, after all, his has only one helipad, not two.

I no longer think my classmate in philosophy class was upset because, without God, her efforts to volunteer meant nothing. Instead, I think she was upset because she volunteered too much. I think she told herself that a good Christian needs to be selfless, which is a lot like saying a strong runner doesn't need water. I think she volunteered every time she was asked and became resentful for missing out on much-needed time with friends. I think she always said yes because rather, than acknowledging her needs, she swallowed her anger and prayed. She prayed for more strength to continue because she needed to do more to help.

I think my classmate suffered from false pride and no matter how many hours she volunteered, it would never be enough. And because of her false pride, I think she thought she was a good Christian, one of the few with the grit to do the Lord's work, but over time came to resent the homeless for always requiring her help. In fact, because of the magnitude of her resentment and pain, she may have secretly believed she was the best Christian in her congregation because none had sacrificed as much as her.

But, that's just my story.

Here's another one. It's about doing enough.

Once upon a time, a woman spoke with a mom who wasn't looking forward to having her adult daughter visit. The daughter was super excited and asked how long she could stay, and the mom, wanting to prove how much she loved her daughter, replied three days. The mom told the woman that three days was the maximum limit she allowed her daughter to stay because, by day three, she was typically ready to strangle her.

In response, the woman asked the mom, "Then why don't you tell your daughter that she can stay only one day? That way you can enjoy your time together, and the next morning, you can send her off with love."

Hmmmm... I wonder if that's what Fredi meant when she said, *to love other people, you first need to love yourself.*

18

DEATH OF A SAINT

"Well, of course your friends think you sound like an asshole, just look at how you describe your ex-wife! You portray her like she's some kind of an angel!"

I'd given Fredi my book for feedback, and she didn't hesitate in providing it.

"You need to describe how vindictive she could be so that your readers get a better picture of the kind of woman she was."

While I could write several chapters about the vengeance my ex-wife unleashed after I had my affair, I didn't perceive her like that before it happened. From what I recall, she was a jovial and carefree person, although as I say that, I did suspect she might have experienced some kind of childhood trauma.

I think it was her reaction to authority figures that made me think that, like when she was stopped by the Nebraska State Patrol for speeding. After the Trooper served her a citation and returned to his car, she released a torrent of obscenities in a red-faced tirade that lasted several minutes long. I have no idea how she managed to string that many expletives together into a single rant but she did. When she finished yelling, she showered the inside of our car with enough tiny fragments of her citation that one might have thought we'd just returned from a Times Square ticker-tape parade.

While I don't know what caused this reaction, I doubt it was the $125 speeding ticket. Judging by her response, her rage was in existence long before that day. And that's when it clicked...

My friend thought I sounded like a jackass at the beginning of this book because I drop my readers into my story just as I'm hurling fireballs of fury at my ex-wife and former boss. At the start of this book, I look like an angry asshole because I'd been letting Sparky pee on my rosebush for the last 25 years and had done nothing to stop it.

Thrilled at having solved this mystery, I wrote to my unemotional friend and described my theory, to which he replied, "No, that wasn't it at all; I understood why you were angry. The reason I thought you were a jerk was because you were manipulating your friend into not bringing his girlfriend along to Europe. You weren't thinking about what your buddy or his girlfriend wanted, all you cared about was you. I called you an asshole because in those first few chapters you come across as a narcissistic prick."

Irritated, I shot back a reply. I explained that I didn't want my buddy to bring his girlfriend because he'd established a track record of becoming so infatuated with his girlfriends, that he'd abandon our friendship for months at a time. Therefore, I was justified in trying to get him to ditch his girlfriend because, just as I'd expected, he did abandon me at that train station in Europe.

Later that night, I woke with the realization that my proofreading friend was right. While my concerns that my buddy would abandon me might have been valid, I'd handled the situation poorly. Rather than telling him that I was afraid he'd abandon me, I'd tried to shame him into leaving his girlfriend at home. I'd used the same kind of passive aggressive approach I'd used with Fredi when I called her car a piece of crap.

I used to think I was a good man, but I was starting to realize that I wasn't. I'd spent the last thirty years behaving like a jackass.

However, as Fredi pointed out in the past: *Most of us assume people are either good or bad, but that's not accurate. People don't wake up thinking "Today I'm going to be an asshole." Instead, they go about their daily lives, largely unaware of how their dysfunctional patterns affect them.*

I used to laugh when she said things like that because, how could someone not know that they're behaving like a jackass? Nevertheless, I'm starting to think that she's right because, I truly didn't know I'd been behaving like that.

While I have written an entire book about how I've lied, judged others unfairly, blamed them for things that weren't their fault, and treated other people like shit, I didn't see myself like that because, that wasn't me. I was the saint. I was that good guy who honored his vows. I was that non-judgmental guy who never got angry and always made it a point to get along with everyone.

Up until this point, you have known me to be a judgmental, angry, insecure, anxious, and inauthentic person who swears like a sailor. The important point to remember, however, is that this is not how I presented myself to the world. You only know these things because I chose to let you into my private thoughts.

Had you met me on the street, you likely wouldn't have thought these things because that's not how I behaved. For example, the me that my ex-wife knew was a loving guy who doted on her and told her how much he loved and cared for her. The me that a stranger met was a slightly shy guy who was kind and respectful and never got mad. The me that my boss knew was a yes man who worked hard and always agreed to work the extra shift. If a person paid attention, they might have seen the real me shine through, like when I had my affair or yelled at the other SWAT team leader, but for the most part, I kept that side of me hidden.

This is why I thought it took grit to be a good person because being a good person meant swallowing my resentment and anger before saying, "Sure, I'd love to donate my change!" Trying to be confident wasn't easy either, because confidence meant pushing through my insecurities to accomplish my goals while pretending that nothing fazed me.

I didn't know it, but without anger and resentment, it's easy to be a good person. And once you mitigate your insecurities, it's easy to feel confident.

I didn't realize I was a jackass because I'd been defining my personality based on my external behaviors, and not by the anger and resentment I was feeling inside.

I thought the saint was me, but he wasn't, he was the avatar I created. He was nothing more than the image I portrayed to the world. He was the mask I wore to show what a calm, kind, and secure person I was. Unfortunately, I'd been wearing that mask for so long I failed to realize I wasn't the saint but the angry, insecure, and judgmental man inside. In other words, I wasn't that nice guy who generously offered you the last cookie, I was the angry man inside who silently cursed you for taking it before offering it back to me.

I didn't think I was an angry person because I didn't allow the saint to behave angry. I didn't know I was so judgmental because I made sure the saint always treated people with fairness and respect. I didn't think I was anxious because I made sure the saint acted like nothing ever bothered him. I was telling myself that, because I acted secure, kind, and respectful, that I was secure, kind, and respectful.

I was so focused on controlling every action of my saintly

avatar that I became disconnected from who I truly was. Fredi refers to this kind of behavior as being out of alignment, because what you do or say is no longer in alignment with how you actually feel inside.

To get myself back into alignment, I needed to stop trying to be the football star who gets all the praise and instead, become that other kid from high school who didn't care what others thought. I needed to become that kid who didn't need compliments to feel good or let criticism make him feel bad. That kid didn't need to prove he was fearless and strong because he loved himself just the way he was. But to love myself like that would be no easy task.

When Fredi challenged my stories, she led me to question everything I knew to be true about myself and the man I'd become. In revealing my dysfunctions, she exposed the saint as a fraud, which left me feeling naked and exposed. Without my saintly image, the man left standing there was my authentic self. It was the man I'd tried so carefully to hide, the man who was resentful, judgmental, and insecure.

What followed was one of the most screwed-up moments in my life. I dumped years' worth of emotions in just a couple of days. I vomited out massive amounts of anger, resentment, and pain. I was sobbing in the shower one minute, pissed off the next, and feeling awesome moments later. It was like some snot-nosed hyperactive kid got loose in my emotional control center and was running around in circles, flipping all the switches.

It was a moment captured perfectly in the movie, *The Peaceful Warrior*. This film, which was based on the book of the same name, tells the story of college gymnast Dan Millman who, in real life, had shattered his leg in a motorcycle accident, thus forcing him to confront the reality that his Olympic dreams might be over. Despondent at the loss of everything he thought himself to be, Dan confronts his alter ego, portrayed as a darker characterization of himself, in a scene that takes place atop a bell tower. He's reached a point where he understands he must let go of his false identity, which is pulling him over the edge by the arms, and as Dan's grip begins to slip, his alter ego screams, "Do you know... who you are... without me?!"

Feeling like everything is collapsing from beneath you is the only way I can describe it. I was letting go of the only person I'd ever known myself to be and losing that self-image had rocked me to the core.

Without the saint, I was reconnecting with my emotions, and after years of neglect, they were in need of some serious calibration. If I wanted to re-align myself and conquer my insecurity, I'd have to start fighting to protect the real me. To feel worthy, I'd have to start treating myself like I *was* worthy. I'd have to stop sacrificing my needs in false acts of kindness, honor, and courage, and start paying attention to my interests instead. I'd have to become comfortable with using my boundaries even at the cost of making others unhappy. In other words, if I really wanted that last cookie, I'd have to take it instead of offering it to someone else.

To honor my true self, I'd have to stop pretending that nothing bothered me, because that's not what an emotionally healthy adult does, but what a child does when he's trying not to cry in front of his father. And suddenly, it all became clear...

I was over forty years old and I was still acting like that same little boy who was attempting to prove to his father that he was strong enough not to cry. That little boy who stood there with a quivering lower lip and watering eyes while trying to ignore his emotions.

I might have looked like a straight-faced SWAT team leader, but on the inside, I was still that little boy trying his best to hide his true feelings. I was still acting like that same little boy who wanted nothing more than to be loved and accepted for who he was. And I hate to say this, because some part of me still thinks I sound like a pussy, but I had to let that little boy cry.

I had to let him know that it was okay to cry and that I would still be there for him when he was done. I had to let him know that it's okay to feel and that I valued him and loved him just the way he was. I had to let him know that no matter what happened he would always be good enough for me. And so, I cried.

At least, that's what I think happened when I vomited up all that anger and resentment and cried in the shower. I was giving that little boy a glass of water and letting him know that he could stop running his marathon so he could drink it. I was letting him know that he no longer needed to prove himself to anyone because he was good enough for me, just the way he was.

By allowing my little boy self to cry without judgment, I was finally standing up for my authentic self. I was letting myself feel the warmth of unconditional love and it felt really, really, really good.

Accepting my true self feels like nothing else in the world. It feels like being unencumbered by worry, concern, and shame, just like that little boy who escapes from his bathtub to run naked through a living room full of dinner guests, giggling all the way, while being chased by his mother holding an outstretched towel. It feels like being proud of my authentic self, irrespective of my flaws, without feeling the need to prove myself or hide any part of me. It feels like allowing me to be me.

My first marathon had been frantic, much like my life, filled with made-up stories and the desire to constantly prove my worth. I must have grown some during that next year because my second marathon felt significantly different.

When I readied myself at the starting line of the Pikes Peak Marathon, Fredi's sister, a seasoned veteran of the race, told me to run as fast as I could to the trailhead before the other runners got there. She explained that the path narrows dramatically once the trailhead is reached making it difficult to pass anyone after that.

I hadn't prepared for this one-mile sprint uphill, and while I beat the majority of the crowd to the trailhead, I was so exhausted when I got there that I was forced to stop to recapture my breath. Panting for several minutes, I watched helplessly as the majority of runners went by.

Just like I'd done in my first marathon, I'd overexerted myself, and it was a blunder that cost me dearly when I got stuck behind a long line of shuffling runners near the top. The steep grade, the thin air at higher altitude, and the narrowing trail had caused this congestion and was the reason Fredi's sister had warned me to get ahead of the pack.

As I began cursing myself for being such a screw-up, an older woman in front of me turned and asked where I came from. She told me she had completed the race several times along with her girlfriends who each year, come from across the US to participate. Before long, I found myself lost in conversation with this woman. No longer worried about the time, my anger and frustration was all but forgotten.

Once I reached the peak, the trail made a hairpin turn onto itself so runners could return down the same path they'd just ascended. The sudden shift from uphill to downhill invigorated my legs and as they stretched into full stride I began darting past other runners. I was running so fast that the cool mountain air rushing past my face felt like I was hanging my head out a car window. Vaulting over rocks and other obstacles I began targeting other contestants, relishing the exhilaration and pride I experienced after passing each one. With my confidence building, I knew I'd easily regain the time I'd lost and would therefore finish much sooner than anticipated.

Thirty minutes later, the air was still as my swollen knees absorbed the impact of yet another downward step on the ankle-twisting root-covered trail. Having only trained for this course uphill, I hadn't anticipated the heavy toll that the steep descent would extract on my body. After my legs buckled for the third time, I transitioned into a hobbling walk to avoid becoming one of the dozen or so casualties each year who tumble down the trail before crossing the finish line in a bloody mess.

It wasn't until I reached the trailhead where, back on pavement, I gave one last push to sprint the final mile home. I crossed the finish line before a crowd of cheering spectators and a large clock that read 8 hours, 35 minutes, and 22 seconds.

I'd done it. I'd completed the Pikes Peak Marathon. After a celebratory dinner with family at a nearby restaurant, where I drank a half dozen shots of ouzo to soothe my sore legs, I went home and looked up the final results of the day. I'd placed in the bottom 25th percentile of all runners, scoring nearly twice as poorly as I'd done in my first marathon.

Had I felt the need to prove myself, I might have hung my head in shame, but there was no need for that. I wasn't embarrassed that all those runners passed me. If anything, I was impressed that they did because that was a brutal race and as far as I'm concerned they kicked ass!

And you know what? So did I. We all kicked ass.

19

IN A WORLD OF MORONS, ASSHOLES, AND ME

Responding to a company post that urged employees to embrace diversity, a woman wrote, "If only we all believed in God, then we'd all get along."

While I'm not sure that history would support her claim, what I wanted to reply was, "Yes, and if we all worshipped Satan and believed we should sacrifice our firstborns in fire, then we'd also, *all get along.*"

But I didn't.

While she may have failed to comprehend the concept of embracing diversity, and thus diverse beliefs, I really can't blame her. That's because, much like her, I have opinions of my own. For instance, I know which brands of cars people should buy, how they should style their hair, and what clothes they should or shouldn't wear in public. I know which hobbies are worthwhile, what values are best, and how other parents should discipline their children. And while this woman thinks we should all believe in God, I disagree because, personally speaking, I'm quite certain God doesn't exist.

The reason I know these things is because, unlike these other people, I'm an intelligent man and actually take the time to think things through. Unfortunately, other people aren't as smart or diligent as me, which is why my world has always been filled with morons...

Or at least, that used to be my story.

What I didn't realize was that I created these morons. In demanding that everyone thinks like me, I created a situation where others must either agree with me or be condemned to the status of moron, but this line of reasoning didn't happen by accident.

In trying to overcome my insecurity, I was subconsciously trying to prove in a variety of ways that I was better than those around me. Instead of searching for ways to connect with others, I was searching for differences by which to judge them, and those differences included the type of car they drove, the way they styled their hair, and the clothes they wore in public. I judged other people for these things because that's how I proved I was the winner.

Interestingly, when you always have to be the winner, then by default, everyone else becomes a loser. I created a world of losers because this is how I felt better about myself. And how do I know this?

Fredi described it like this: *When you're insecure, you need affirmation that what you believe is true. So, you either need people to agree with your view of the world, or you need to find a reason why they don't, and what simpler way to explain why they don't than to declare them stupid, misguided, or misinformed?*

When Fredi said you can't love other people until you first love yourself, she was right. I was never going to love any of these morons until I addressed my insecurity issues, which is what happened near the end of my chapter titled, *ME BIG MAN, ME WEAR BIG CONDOM*. I didn't realize it when I wrote that chapter, but the reason I felt connected to other people was because... I no longer needed them to be like me.

If loving yourself means allowing yourself to be who you are without judgment, then it only makes sense that loving other people happens by allowing them to be who they are without judgment. And that is what loving myself has allowed me to do.

A few months ago, a Christian friend told me about the day he realized that the only logical explanation for the existence of the universe was that it had been intelligently designed by God. As he described the thrill he felt at finally understanding the origin of himself and everything around him, I felt no need to roll my eyes, question his belief in God, or challenge his theory of creationism with my theory of evolution. The only thing I felt was acceptance for him and happy that he was excited by his newfound discovery.

In standing up for myself and becoming confident in who I am, I have become secure in my beliefs and no longer worry what others think. In a twisted and unexpected way, this ability to not give a crap what other people think has allowed me to connect with those I previously considered morons. Since I no longer care what they think, they are free to think whatever they want, and so rather than judging them, I now see them simply as people with different beliefs.

Without the need to share beliefs, I'm connecting with others through our shared experiences instead. I felt excited for my Christian friend's discovery because I know what it feels like to be excited by a new discovery. Instead of judging a kid for wanting to pull buffelgrass from the desert, I can now share in his feelings of camaraderie he experiences with other people instead. In understanding what it feels like to be afraid, I can appreciate the fear that someone might experience when confronting a spider, even though spiders don't scare me.

I believe they call this type of shared experience, empathy, and that learning to love myself was the key that finally unlocked this ability within me. And now that I have experienced it, I'm pretty sure that empathy is the meaning of life because, in sharing experiences with others, I no longer see all these other people as different. In essence, empathy has made all these morons much easier to love. However, it's not only the morons that are easier to love, but the assholes too.

The assholes are those dysfunctional and inauthentic types who have acted much like I have throughout this book. They're the ones who have lied to me, judged me, unfairly, blamed me for making them angry, and treated me poorly without telling me why because they were wearing their face of fear.

For instance, if I mistakenly call a woman a she, when she wants to be known by the pronoun he, and he becomes unglued and starts yelling at me for addressing him by the wrong pronoun, then I would have previously thought of him as an asshole for yelling at me.

In the past, I would have taken this response personally. I would have either apologized profusely for being so inconsiderate or snapped back aggressively, "How in the hell am I supposed to know what you want to be called?"

Fredi has shown me that I don't have to become upset or take these attacks personally, because his reaction isn't about me. I wasn't acting with malice, nor did I have any intention of being disrespectful, and, rather than yelling at me, he could have simply corrected me. After all, had he called me a "she", I probably would have just laughed.

The reason this person got upset was not because I called him by the wrong pronoun, but because of the stories he made up in his head. He was blaming me for making him angry. He got upset because I *should* have known what to call him, because I *should* have asked how he wanted to be addressed, or maybe because I *shouldn't* have disrespected him for his choice of pronoun.

It's kind of like calling someone overweight; I might get a

wide range of reactions. One person might say, "yeah, I know, but look how sexy I am!", while the next might talk about the disappointment she feels that none of her diets have helped. One might get angry while lashing out, "Fuck you, stick boy!", while another might break down in a puddle of tears and feelings of worthlessness.

I didn't cause these different reactions, their stories did. If I'd intended to be demeaning or rude, then I might need to apologize, but I didn't do that.

By addressing my insecurity I've learned that I don't have to defend myself against another person's triggered behavior because their reaction isn't about me.

Instead, I can decide whether or not to accept their response. If I choose not to accept it, then I can simply reply with compassion, "OK, thanks for letting me know which pronoun you use, I'll try to remember that next time."

I used to live in a world filled with morons and assholes, but not anymore. Now I live in a world filled with ordinary people who are more or less just like me. Occasionally, some of them behave like assholes but I don't take it personally anymore. I know they're acting like that, not because they're bad people, but because they're just feeling a little angry, insecure, or scared.

And that's okay, because occasionally, despite my best efforts, I still get triggered myself, and when I do, I can behave like an asshole too.

20

SHITSTORMS CAUSED BY SHOULD

Over the years, Fredi has told me of patients who were riddled with anxiety over something they felt and upset because they thought they *shouldn't* feel that way. After echoing her patients' concerns back, she'd often ask, "But why wouldn't you feel that way? I would think it odd if you didn't!" In a matter of minutes, she'd often see her patients' bodies and expressions relax as they began to comprehend that their feelings were normal given their current circumstances.

I mentioned in an earlier chapter that *should* was forged in hell by Satan himself, and while I don't believe in Satan, I love the image of this thick horned massive evil dude hammering away on a molten iron *should*. I like this association because, not only is *should used to indicate obligation, duty, or correctness, typically when criticizing someone's actions* (as Oxford's Dictionary defined it), but because *should* creates the expectation that reality *should* somehow be different from what it is.

In the case of Fredi's patients, much of their anxiety was generated, not by what they were feeling, but by their belief they *shouldn't* be feeling it. It was their *should* that created their distress by creating an alternate reality where they shouldn't be feeling what they felt. In fact, her patients weren't even able to address their underlying issues until Fredi helped them dispel this false reality and accept their situation for what it was.

I experienced this same issue myself. When I told myself I *shouldn't* be fearful on the SWAT team, I created an alternate reality where SWAT team members are fearless, and therefore any fear whatsoever was an indication of ineptness. Rather than accepting my fears were a normal response to a dangerous situation, which would have allowed me to focus my attention on the mission, I became obsessed with the slightest signs of nervousness and was thereafter haunted by thoughts of inadequacy. A similar situation occurred when I told myself that I *should* have the arms of a bodybuilder and the cock of a pornstar, or when I told myself that I should have more endurance than a woman with a big bottom. In all these situations, my self-imposed *shoulds* created a reality with expectations that I was unable to meet, which was the direct cause of the shame and humiliation I experienced.

In other cases, like when I said I *shouldn't* stop running during my marathon, or that I *should* honor my vows to my ex-wife, I created expectations that compelled me to alter what would have otherwise been my authentic response. Instead of stopping and getting water, I became dangerously dehydrated, and instead of telling my ex-wife the truth, I became unreasonably infuriated with her.

My self-imposed *shoulds* and their resulting expectations had not only caused me shame but pain and anger as well. But it wasn't just my self-imposed *shoulds* that caused problems, but the *shoulds* I imposed on others.

When I claimed my wife *shouldn't* make plans without asking me first, my boss *shouldn't* ask me to work the extra shift, or my Christian friend *shouldn't* believe in God, I created a reality in which these people were unable to live up to my expectations. I was justified in blaming them, hating them, and shaming them because they weren't behaving as they *should*. Unfortunately, I had so many *shoulds* and expectations in my self-created reality that very few people could meet my criteria of acceptable behavior, which is exactly why I lived in a world of morons and assholes.

When Fredi kept asking me to question my stories, she was teaching me to question the judgments I made of others and myself. In getting me to question my judgments of others, she challenged my expectations of their behavior, which essentially destroyed my framework of *shoulds*. No longer able to live in my world of *should*, I was forced to live in the world as it actually is.

In the world that is, there are no *shoulds* or expectations, because things are simply just the way they are. If I run a marathon without expectations of where I *should* place, then it doesn't matter if I finish in the top or bottom 25th percentile.

In this world, if I don't like something, it's up to me to change it. Without the expectation of whether my boss *should* have asked me to work the extra shift, *should* know better than to ask, or that I *shouldn't* have to tell him that he's treating me unfairly, I can simply say "no". Without expectations that Fredi *should* put down her phone so that we can talk before I leave for work, I no longer have to feel upset if she doesn't, I can simply ask if she will. And perhaps most importantly, without the expectation that a driver *should not* cut me off in traffic, I no longer need to feel offended when he does.

Fredi once said that, *people expect the world should be fair and that they shouldn't have to experience negative emotions. Unfortunately, these kinds of shoulds create a false expectation of how reality actually is, which therefore leads to hate, blame, and anger.*

When I lived in the world of *shoulds* and expectations, I was living in a state of denial. It was a world where things *shouldn't* have happened, *should* have been done differently, or *shouldn't* have been as they were. And that's the problem with *should*, it's absolute. With should, there are no exceptions. And maybe that's why my unemotional friends can't accept the things I've done. Because no matter the reason, I *shouldn't* have tried to manipulate my friend, I *shouldn't* have had an affair, I *should* have raised my son better, or I *shouldn't* have done... whatever. Unfortunately, there is no room for forgiveness in a world of *should, only the fact that you should or shouldn't have done what you did.*

Now that I live in the world that actually is, I like it much better. In this world, everyone is free to be themselves, and all I'm required to do is protect my boundaries. It makes for a much simpler world because I no longer need to wait for others to do what they should or shouldn't do, I just do what's right for me.

Do you know what I think we *should* do? We *should* get rid of *should*. Yeah... that's what we *should* do, we *should* get rid of *should*.

PART IV

THE LEARNING
NEVER ENDS

21

MA, I'M NOT GAY

"It's okay if you're gay," my mother told me, "I will always love you, no matter what."

"Ma, I'm not gay, I just want to stay at my friend's house."

"But didn't you say your friend *might* be gay?" she asked, as if needing to confirm what I just said.

"Well, yeah, he might be, but he's still my friend and I told him I would stay; besides, I haven't seen him in a long time."

"Well, okay... I just want you to know that I love you... even..."

"Ma! I'm not gay!"

There really was no question about it, my friend was definitely gay; he looked gay, he talked gay, he was gay. The thing about my gay friend is that he had a straight girlfriend who lived across the street, and this girlfriend had another girlfriend who would come over to visit, and the two of them liked to skinny dip together regardless of whether my gay friend watched.

I met my friend a couple of years earlier in junior high school. We rode the bus together, and one day he told me about the naked girls. I decided a friendship was in order. He invited me to come over and meet them, and sure enough, these girls liked to skinny dip, and while they were at it, they expressed their desire to get laid as well.

They suggested I have sex with them, and since a condom was unavailable, I could use a balloon instead. While I thought this was a splendid idea, I couldn't do it. The problem was that girls in junior high school tend to look like fully developed young women while the males of their same age still resemble little boys. Desperately awaiting the arrival of my first pubic hair, I was too embarrassed to reveal my young boy nakedness and therefore declined their generous offer of sex.

It was a decision I came to regret heavily when our family moved out of state.

A few years had passed since then, and I was eager to give this summer fantasy another try, even at the cost of my mother thinking me gay. It wasn't until the second day of my two-day visit that we connected with the girl who lived across the street, and as she settled on my lap and began grinding her hips atop my jeans, I knew my good fortune had returned.

Prior to leaving for this trip, I obtained a condom that I had hidden inside a cassette tape that I had left in my friend's bedroom. When I say inside the cassette, I mean that I took out the screws, removed the rolled-up tape, covered the tiny viewing window with black electrical tape to make it look like the original was still there, and carefully packaged the condom inside. At my age, a condom was considered contraband. Not only did I have to protect my parents from the notion that I might have sex, but imagine what my mother would have thought had she discovered it as I left to spend the night at my gay friend's house.

"I have a condom," I whispered into the young woman's ear.

Grinding down harder, she replied, "Go get it; get it now."

I dashed across the street while thanking the Gods that my plight as a virgin was finally over. Once at my friend's house, I ripped open the cassette tape, grabbed the condom, and was halted at my friend's bedroom door by his mother who now blocked my passage to manhood.

"I'm so glad you're back," she said, "it's time for dinner."

Oh, for fuck sake! Really? Now?

I swallowed my spaghetti and meatballs and washed them down with a gulp of water. I pushed off the table, and just as I began to stand, the doorbell of my wretched fate began to chime.

My parents arrived to take me home.

"It's time to go." my dad said.

"Ok, fine." I told him, "But before we do, she's waiting, my friend, across the street, we were going to..., but then..., umm..., I've got to say goodbye."

My mind was doing the math as I sprinted across the dining room floor. S*ex only took a minute, right? I just had to pull down her pants and put it in. Hell, I could do that in 30 seconds, then what? Maybe another 20 or 30 to finish up? No problem, I'll be back in a flash! Look out baby, here I come!*

"We don't have time." my dad said as he trapped me mid-flight against the living room wall, "It's a long drive and we need to get going."

Looking over his shoulder, I could see her bedroom window through the open front door. The blinds were closed, but she was there, right now, waiting, probably in bed, naked. This was unfathomable; sex was waiting for me behind that window and all I had to do was cross the street. I looked at my friend, desperate for help, but he just shrugged.

And just like that, my virginity returned with a vengeance.

How could this have happened? The timing of these events was too precise. Did my friend play a role in this catastrophe? Did he call my parents? Was he jealous? Was he pissed off because he thought I was coming to see him? Had I unknowingly destroyed his fantasy of getting laid as well? And had he secreted a condom in his room that was meant for me?

Interestingly, I never thought of my friend's predicament until I typed that just now. The only thing that ever mattered to me, was me. I never thought about other people, how they might be feeling, or how I might have misled my friend to get at his girlfriend. And was he even a friend, or just a tool I used to get what I wanted? Because to be honest, I don't remember much about him, not even his last name, but I do remember hers...

Was that because he was gay?

I always thought I was okay with gay. I mean, I've made some gay jokes in my time, but I've also had gay friends, although it was only one, and she was a girl. However, I voted for gay rights, and always made it a point to be welcoming and friendly to the gay people I've met. But does any of that mean I'm okay with gay?

A few years back, Fredi and I attended the Territory Days Festival in Old Colorado City. It's a street fair meant to celebrate the old west, but like most such events, has become dominated by rows of pop-up tents occupied by artists and vendors selling everything from scented body soaps to cell phone service. As we made our way through the crowded street, we passed a booth occupied by a local LGBT group. A woman at the booth caught Fredi's attention and the two of them began to chat.

As their conversation ensued, with no end in sight, I found myself getting fidgety. There were a lot of people walking by and I began calculating the odds that I might know one of them. I was quite certain that it wouldn't be long and wondered what they would think if they saw me standing in front of this booth.

I put my arm around Fredi and stood there for a minute, but the uncomfortable fidgety feeling remained. Gently, I began pulling her sideways by her hip, but she didn't budge. As I pulled at her a second time, I whispered, "Honaaay, let's keep walkiiiiing." It was no use; she was deep in conversation. Slowly, I drifted away, fading into the crowd, drawn in by an unexplored interest in the ladybug refrigerator magnets stuck on the side of a nearby booth.

Unlike me, Fredi has never cared what people think. She wears an Apple watch with a rainbow strap because she likes the vibrant colors.

"Honey, you know that people will think you're gay if you wear that, right?"

She smiled, "Yeah, I guess they might."

"But they'll think you're gay!" I repeated, just in case she didn't hear me.

"Yeah, it's true. But I like it. It's pretty."

The point is, she doesn't care. Just like my son didn't care when he was four years old and I asked him what he wanted to wear, and he told me he wanted to wear his rainbow belt.

"How about the black one instead?" I asked, "Black is nice. Don't you think the black one's nice?"

"No Daddy, I like my rainbow belt!"

"Fine! Wear your rainbow belt! But hold on for a second; let's untuck your shirt."

Of course, none of this would matter if I didn't have a problem with gay. If someone mistook me for being a truck driver, or a lawyer, it wouldn't faze me much. But if they thought I was gay, now that would be a different story! I'd probably go into a long explanation of why I love boobs, and women, and would make an overt complaint about the close-talking naked men who inhabit every men's locker room. Some might claim my paranoia is a symptom of being uncomfortable with my sexuality and that perhaps deep inside my subconscious, I have a hidden desire to be gay, but I'm pretty sure that's not the case.

I've read books by gay authors and one of them talked about his attraction to a man's hairy arms, and I can honestly say that I find nothing attractive about a man's hairy arms, his hairy face, or his hairy ass. For me, it's always been about the boobs. As my drunk friend once texted, "Gawd, I love boobs. Everything about them. Boobs, boobs, boobs!" That makes sense to me. It's been that way since I was a little boy. I used to masturbate to the cartoon sketches of naked women occasionally drawn by Sergio Aragones in the margins of MAD magazine; it was the only porn available to me at the time. Barely a half-inch tall, these images were slightly more detailed than a shapely stick figure with two circles for breasts, but it didn't matter, something about the roundness of those circles always excited the hell out of me.

But this speaks to the great gift Fredi has imparted on me. No longer do I feel squeamish about such unexplained feelings, I start diving into them. What's driving them? Where are they coming from? What story am I telling myself?

I'm guessing my gay issues come from growing up in the '80s. The standard insult at the time was to call someone a fag or a homo, and jokes at the expense of gay folk were common. I remember being so careful not to do anything that made me look gay. What that means, I don't know anymore, but at the time it looked like any guy who behaved a little too effeminate, talked with a lisp, walked with his hand bent at the wrist, or listened to music by artists suspected of being gay. And that was the level of paranoia I lived with, you didn't have to be gay, you just had to be suspected of being gay.

And this is precisely why I was so paranoid about being associated with gay. Because you can't see gay. Gay can look like anyone. Sometimes it's flamboyant and shows itself proudly, and at other times it's hidden and looks like a grocery clerk, a dentist, or maybe a tall guy standing at an LGBT tent at the Territory Days Festival in Old Colorado City. That's what makes gay so dangerous, it's invisible, and if I was labeled as such, there would be no way to prove it wasn't true. I'm guessing that's why they developed those *straight but not narrow* t-shirts, for people like me. People who want to say, I'm here to support you, as long as no one thinks I'm anything like you.

I'm skeptical of anyone who says they don't have any stereotypes or biases; I believe everyone does in some capacity or another. It's human nature. I saw that frequently as a cop. Many people talk about the stereotypes that cops in the United States have against African Americans and other minorities, but it goes the other way too. I arrested a guy for theft one time, and he shouted out to the crowd that I was only arresting him because he was black. "No", I answered, "I arrested you because you and your family stuffed 500 dollars' worth of lobsters down the front of your pants." It was a no-brainer; the surveillance video showed them doing it. He just said that to create a scene and get me off his back.

However, in many cases, my reason for contacting the person wasn't as clear and I was simply assumed to be a racist because I wore a badge. I would contact a person for a legitimate reason and because of their racist assumptions, they'd become confrontational with me. But that's what biases do. These folks had no idea how hard I tried to treat everyone equally. They didn't see all the times that I didn't act and chose to walk away instead. They weren't there to see me educating the white lady that I wouldn't be contacting the "suspicious black man in the park" because there was nothing "suspicious" about a black man walking his dog in the park.

But the first step to changing stereotypes is admitting that they are there, and then being open to talk about them while discussing and questioning their origins. Open discussion is the key to understanding, and that's what I would try to do. I knew these folks were triggered by the badge. It had nothing to do with me, I just walked up and said hello. So, I'd give them a few minutes to decompress and then take the time to explain my reasons for the contact. Once they saw my reasoning, they often apologized for jumping to conclusions.

This is not to say that I don't have any racial prejudices at all. When I first became a cop, the recruits were required to take a Latino diversity class. I didn't think I needed a class like that, but I did. I was surprised when the instructor mentioned that most Mexican migrants don't want to come to America. "Would you want to leave your family, your home, and your friends to go to a country where you don't speak the language only to work a crappy job that no one else wants?" the instructor asked. "Migrants don't want to be here; they're just trying to make enough money to help their family survive back home."

I was a young cop at the time, but those few sentences completely changed my perspective on the matter. Even to this day, I think about those words when I see refugees who are trying to escape the murder and rape that's terrorizing their homeland. Many countries try to shut these migrants out, calling them greed-seeking freeloaders, but wouldn't I be doing the same thing if my homeland was overrun by terrorists?

When a presidential candidate said he wanted to "make America great again", I thought it sounded like an excellent slogan for a politician to use. My mind pictured the nineteen fifties when the U.S. economy was growing, and people seemed to have bright futures. I thought of those pretty little homes with their manicured lawns you see in the movies representing the era. That generation knew style; their cars were so sleek, and I loved the way they dressed. The men wore those broad-shouldered suits with narrow ties, and the women wore those colorful dresses that hugged their figures and looked so pretty.

Yeah, let's do it! Let's make America great again!

Soon after, I heard a story on the radio giving the African-American perspective on the matter. The commentator said, "We've spent the last 70 years fighting for the freedom to sit in the front of a bus, to eat at good restaurants, to attend any school, and finally, after more than 200 years, we just saw our first black president, and now you want to make America great again?" I cringed; it never occurred to me how that little phrase could have such different meanings to different people living in the same nation.

These days I play the trading places game with myself; it helps me gain perspective. I ask myself, what if the roles were reversed? What if heterosexuality was considered abnormal? Would I sleep with a man just to conform to society's standards? Would I be considered a freak because I fell in love with a woman? Would there be anything different about me as a person, or in how I raised my children, because of who I was attracted to? No, I'd still be the same person.

We should be free to love, enjoy, and be with anyone we want. There's no shame in being gay or in any of the other categories expressed by LGBT. Nor is there any shame in standing at a booth with an LGBT banner hung over it. And really, there's no shame in having stereotypes, we all have them. It is a shame, however, if we choose to let those stereotypes continue to shape our behavior when we are afforded the opportunity to change.

A few months ago, my computer crashed at work. The repair technician, Steve, told me over the phone to meet him in the hallway so I'd be easier to find. Before hanging up, he mentioned that I'd know him when I saw him. As I waited, a slim woman in a tight mini-skirt approached, quite good-looking I might add, and as she got closer, I realized this was Steve. I stood behind him as he worked on my computer and studied him. I was baffled at how feminine he looked; he really was attractive. I told Fredi about my experience with Steve, that he was the best computer tech that ever worked on my computer, and asked whether she thought Steve would want me to address him as *he* or *she*. I even told others about my experience with Steve and admitted that I thought he was an attractive woman..., man..., man-woman. I said this without paranoia, without having to explain myself, and without worrying whether my sexuality would be called into question. This was a big step for me.

I saw Steve a few weeks later at work. It was in a huge room filled with hundreds of cubicles arranged in sections marked by columns and rows. However, this wasn't just any office space, this was the engineering lab. These cubes were occupied by intelligent people, some of the brightest in the nation, and as they diligently worked in their assigned cubicles to solve their technically complex problems, it came as no surprise to me I saw Steve. The same Steve who, having embraced the *bring your whole self to work* policy was now walking down the main aisle in a white ballerina outfit. With his every step, his tutu gently bounced, as the large star atop his magic wand swung back and forth with his arms. I assumed Steve brought his magic wand to banish viruses from the computers he fixed that day, and that he likely made a "bing" noise each time he tapped his wand on the device to signal the owner that his work was done.

Steve knows who he is and he's proud of it. He was having fun that day and while I'm sure that he knew his outfit would get some laughs, that didn't stop him. There's no shame in him, which I think is pretty cool. I don't know much about Steve, but if I did, I think I would be glad to call him a friend. Or should I say, I'd be glad to call *her* a friend?

Someday I'll volunteer to sit at an LGBT tent and hand out brochures. Maybe I'll do it in a town where I know lots of people, and I won't even wear one of those *straight but not narrow* T-shirts.

Yeah..., that's what I'll do... someday... but not yet... maybe... we'll see...

22

A HEALTHY KIND OF SELFISH

"What do you think of these pants?"

Ok, I know dudes aren't supposed to enjoy shopping for clothes with their wives, but I love it. I think Fredi looks hot. So, when she comes out of a dressing room and struts around in some cute little outfit, I rather enjoy it. And because I enjoy it, the last thing I want to do is waste my time watching her walk around in something that looks bad. That's why I have no problem telling her the truth.

On this particular day, she had put on a pair of the grooviest pants I'd ever seen. Splattered in bright colors, these suckers hugged her hips and thighs before flaring out into massively wide bell bottoms. I'll admit, they looked great on her ass, but oh my god, the thought of walking around in public with her in these clown pants was simply too much to ask.

"Honey! Take those off before anyone sees us! What the hell are you thinking?"

She turned, looked in the mirror, rocked her hips from side to side, and replied, "Really? I like 'em. I think I'll buy 'em."

Well, that wasn't supposed to happen. She asked what I thought, I said no, and now she was supposed to hang the pants back on the rack. That's what people in relationships do; they respect each other's desires.

The same thing happened when she legally changed her name to Fredi. Fredi comes from her middle name, Alfreda. Her family had always called her Freda, but her friends had dubbed her Fredi. So, when she decided to change her name to Fredi, I urged her to reconsider. Fredi sounded too masculine to me and I didn't want anyone to think I was sleeping with a dude. But did she listen?

Nope.

Not too long ago, she opened a hypnotherapy office. She's an awesome psychiatrist who has helped change countless lives during her career. Unfortunately, some psychiatrists have poor boundaries and prescribe whatever medications their patients want, while others don't take the time to conduct a full assessment and create an accurate diagnosis, thereby condemning their patients to a regimen of medications they don't require. Because of this, Fredi occasionally has to wean her patients off medications that were either prescribed in dangerous combinations or that were unsuitable for their condition. In many cases, the patient was simply suffering from one of the many dysfunctional thought patterns I've already described and didn't even require medications in the first place. I always appreciated the work she's done, because as a psychiatrist, she excels at helping people improve their lives.

However, Fredi and her sisters lean a bit toward the metaphysical side and believe in some of the more holistic treatments and therapies that don't necessarily sit well with my logical brain. That's why when she starts talking about hypnosis and such, I'll start singing my little song that goes, "You and your sisters are nuts, nuts, nuts..." She smiles, but it doesn't change anything. She still does what she wants.

To me, it just doesn't seem right. It's like she doesn't care. If she cared, then she'd do these things for me, right?

We talked about my need for her to do things for me, and this is what she had to say. *"Happiness comes from being aligned with your authentic self. It comes from being and protecting yourself with healthy boundaries, and by seeking out others who support you for who you are."*

Once again, she was right. I wasn't respecting her choices, instead, I was asking her to caretake me, and I was pretty sure I knew why.

My mom was a joy to be around, but when my dad came home from work, that's when she'd transform into her role of a 1950s housewife whose sole purpose was to care for her husband's needs. As the man of the house, he expected his slippers to be at the front door, his three children to be quiet so that he could take a nap, and his dinner to be ready once he awoke. After dinner, he expected his wife to clean up and take care of the kids so that he could disappear into his office until it was time for bed. Occasionally, he'd help us with our homework, or yell down the stairs that we were being too loud, but other than that, we rarely spent time with our father.

Not long after my mom died, my father described their relationship perfectly. After admitting that he had taken our mother for granted, he asked in a forlorn voice, "Who's going to cook and clean for me now?"

I don't think I ever considered the extent to which my parent's relationship had affected me, but with an absent father, I was raised by a mother who would serve as a blueprint for relationships. She taught me the analytics of determining my spouse's needs and fulfilling those needs before being asked. She taught me how to place my spouse's needs ahead of my own, and that caretaking is how one expresses love.

Caretaking has been at the threshold of almost every topic in this book. Caretaking is why I always let my first wife have her way, why I waited for my father before eating at Thanksgiving, and even how I tried not to offend other people. I had been contorting myself around the needs and desires of others, trying to make their lives better and less stressful, while neglecting my own needs in the process.

Caretaking doesn't nurture love, it nurtures anger and resentment, and while I'm keenly aware of this fact, it still hasn't been an easy lesson for me to learn.

I asked Fredi why it was so difficult for me to stand up for myself and stop caretaking the feelings of others. She responded: *standing up for yourself requires you to make decisions that will often make others unhappy. And that's a tough thing to do when you've spent a lifetime trying to make all those same people happy.*

Learning to protect my boundaries, by putting my interests ahead of those that I love, is something that initially felt... selfish.

When I returned to my mistress and discovered that she was no longer perfect, I began to realize how twisted my previous relationships had been. With my first wife, I'd locked myself into the relationship because I shamed myself into honoring my vows. Then, with my mistress, I surreptitiously tried to keep her at home and contemplated marrying her because I feared she'd leave me for another man.

Figuratively speaking, I had unwillingly fenced myself into my first marriage and then tried to fence in my mistress during my affair. These, of course, were boundary violations, wherein the first I failed to enforce my boundaries, while in the second I attempted to violate those of my mistress. And when I started to think about all these fences and boundaries, my mind naturally turned to horses.

Have you ever seen two horses that are in different pastures separated by a fence, yet choose to stand together whenever they can? The fence doesn't prevent either from walking away, but it does prevent one from imposing their will on the other. The horses are free to come and go and behave how they please, yet they choose to stand side by side because that's where they want to be.

The image of these two horses standing together was etched in my mind and got me thinking about marriage. I thought about how I felt trapped in my first marriage because of my wedding vows with no hope of escape but death. Then, I thought about how I considered asking my mistress to marry me to keep her from running away. With these thoughts, I began to see marriage as a chain. I found myself asking the question, why would I even want to stay with someone if they didn't want to be with me? That's not love; that's just being selfish. I want someone who loves me and wants to be with me. I want someone who is happy and enjoys who I am. And if I want to be with them, and they want to be with me, then why does there need to be a chain to keep us together?

That day, I decided that I would never commit myself to a lover, nor would I accept a commitment from a lover, ever again. This concept of no commitments thrilled me. It thrilled me because everyone would know that each day Fredi and I stayed together, we were doing so out of our own free will. Fredi would know that no matter what pants she wears, what medical philosophy she believes in, what name she uses, what sickness she has, or what argument we get into, I'm standing next to her because that's where I'm choosing to be. I want her to know that there is absolutely nothing that keeps me from loving, desiring, or screwing another woman because that way she knows I'm choosing not to do those things because I want to be with her.

That, to me, is love.

So, I shared my vision with Fredi. I described the green grass in the pasture, the white picket fence, and the two lovely horses standing side by side. Her reply came quick and fast.

"Bullshit!"

She doesn't want to stand in a pasture; she wants commitment. She wants to know that I'll fight for our relationship. She wants to know that I'll stay by her side when times get tough and that I won't run off with some darling half her age.

While she believes that I have a fear of marriage that I haven't dealt with, it doesn't feel that way to me. In my mind, the image of these horses makes perfect sense, and that's the only thing that really matters because I need to take care of myself. And so, while the caretaker in me desperately wants to give in, I refuse to do it because I know I'll resent her if I do, and I just can't let that happen.

To this day, I still haven't given her a ring, nor have I asked her to marry me. Although we are technically married by the laws of the State of Colorado, a legal consequence of living together and utilizing each other's benefits, I have remained steadfast in my refusal to commit.

We've been together for over fifteen years now, making it the longest relationship I've ever been in. This leaves me with only one thing to say.

I'm thankful.

I'm thankful for each day I wake up to find her sleeping next to me. I'm thankful because I know that, each day I find her there, she has chosen to stay with me, even if only, for one more day.

23

THE JOB THAT WASN'T MEANT TO BE

I knew a man once who worked for the Census Bureau. It was his job to contact people at home and determine how many lived in the residence. He took his job seriously and worked hard; he wanted his count of the population to be as accurate as possible. If someone wasn't home, he'd return time and again, because he knew the importance of having the most accurate count.

The man's coworker wasn't as diligent. If no one was home, he might peek over the fence to see if there was a swing set or some kind of indication of how many people lived there but would then scribble in an estimate before moving on to the next house.

The man I knew had no respect for his co-worker; he thought of the man's guesswork as unprincipled and sloppy.

Toward the end of the counting season, the supervisor announced a promotion was soon to occur. The man I knew dearly wanted the position, and so he worked harder and longer to demonstrate that he was the obvious choice. However, the supervisor chose to promote his coworker, which confounded the man I knew. "How could they have chosen him," he asked out loud, "the guy's count is way off!"

The answer was simple. His supervisor valued efficiency over accuracy.

I mentioned earlier that when I was trying to become a police officer, I'd go to the various agencies and learn everything I could before testing. I did this, because police departments have wildly different cultures depending on what they value, and so I wanted to know how best to respond to their questions. And when I got into the interviews, I wanted them to know I could do anything they required of me so that they knew I was the best candidate for the job.

I also read in some job guides that when asked about a weakness, I should present a strength instead, but disguise it to look like a weakness. For instance, my weakness is that I prefer to do things correctly and accurately, so sometimes it takes me a little longer to complete my assignments. That sure sounds a lot better than admitting I suck at multitasking!

Fredi later explained that my diligence was setting me up for failure. I was pretending to value things I didn't. And while it was true that I might get the job, I'd likely end up in a job that wasn't right for me. In other words, I'd be like the man who valued an accurate count, who worked for a boss who didn't.

She reminded me that we spend the majority of our lives at work, which is why it's so important to find one that fits your personality. When our values and skills align with the organization's, we tend to be motivated and enjoy the work, which leads to recognition and praise for who we are. It's a snowball effect that keeps tumbling in a positive direction.

When I first met Fredi, I was in the process of quitting my job in law enforcement to start my own business. I invested all of my retirement funds from the police department to start *The Safer Spot*. It was a business designed to legitimize private sales made on Craigslist and Facebook Marketplace, by offering a safe place to transact while providing extra services like vehicle and jewelry inspections to help prevent fraud. I opened my doors a month before the housing crisis of 2008, and within two years, I lost everything, including my home.

Broke, and badly in need of an income, I applied to various police departments since that was the fastest way back to a viable paycheck. But each time I applied, I complained to Fredi about having to return to law enforcement. I'd enjoyed it as a younger man, but after 15 years, I'd burned myself out.

"Why don't you do something else?" she asked, "Maybe you could go back to school?"

That was something I hadn't considered. Although I dropped out of school the first time, I suspected my poor performance was largely driven by immaturity and a lack of motivation. The more I thought about returning to school, the more excited I became.

To help me narrow down a career field, Fredi asked, "When do you lose yourself in your work? What kind of tasks are you doing when you become so absorbed that time just seems to fly by?"

It was an easy question to answer. I loved writing the SWAT plans; they were so complex. I loved the 3-dimensional aspects of the problem. My mind imagined all the different places that a suspect could hide and where our team would be vulnerable or bottlenecked. I had to consider the angles of gunfire and where the bullets would land if they traveled through walls. If we used chemical gas, I had to decide where to insert it, where the suspect would go as a result, and in what direction the wind would carry the venting gas. Even the time of day played a role. It told us in which part of the house we'd likely encounter the suspect or whether a school might let out during our operation and flood the neighborhood with children.

I loved SWAT, but I also loved the serious and fatal accident investigations as well. These were the high-value accidents where court judgments could add up to millions of dollars. We had to account for all the damage on the cars to identify exactly what happened, otherwise, some slick-talking lawyer could propose an alternate theory to muddle up the case. And that's not an easy thing to do, as these collisions were complex with multiple vehicles bouncing around like pinballs. We'd sit around for hours in a conference room, simulating the accident with Matchbox cars to figure out what happened, and slowly investigators would give up and walk away. I always remained, loving the challenge, and relishing that moment when the different pieces of evidence suddenly clicked into place.

It was solving complex problems that turned me on; that's what I love to do!

"Look at the course catalog of the local university," Fredi suggested, "and see what stands out to you."

I did, and it didn't take long to see the engineering degrees were the ones that caught my attention. Software engineering seemed interesting, but I zeroed in on mechanical because of its diversity. Mechanical engineers learn about fluids, structures, thermodynamics, material properties, and electronics, not to mention drawing complex parts and systems in 3-D. It seemed like mechanical engineers did a little bit of everything!

And that's how I went back to school in my mid-40s to become a mechanical engineer.

To get discounted tuition, I applied for a job as a maintenance mechanic at the local university. There were over 100 applicants, many of whom were tradesmen older than me, and after taking a skills test, I was one of only three to be asked back for an interview. Excited, I told Fredi, who suggested an alternative plan.

"Why don't I work", she said, "and you go back to school full time? That way it will be faster to get you back into a decent-paying job."

It was a good plan. We sold almost everything we owned and rented a tiny house that was filled with cockroaches, but in four years, I walked out of school with both bachelor's and master's degrees in mechanical engineering.

With my diplomas in hand, she suggested I look at some jobs and pick out the top three that appealed to me. There were so many that sounded interesting, but the modeling and simulation jobs kept catching my attention. Engineers in this field build models of physical systems in software. These models are used for testing, analysis, and driving changes to the design of actual systems. To me, it didn't sound like a job, but more like fun.

The aerospace companies are highly innovative and often solve some of the hardest problems, so that's where I focused my attention. As I started to apply, it didn't take long to discover that the local companies were looking for electrical and software engineers, but not the mechanical types. To compound the problem, my school had graduated far more mechanical engineers than any other. As I began interviewing, the desire to tell the recruiters whatever they wanted to hear seemed like the obvious choice, after all, I needed a paycheck.

Instead, I took Fredi's advice and told them the truth. I told them what I did well, and what I didn't do well. I told them what I liked to do, and what I didn't like to do. And even when I knew I was about to say something that would cut my chances of getting the job, I still said it.

The strangest thing then happened. They listened and heard me. They began to understand who I was. And even though they told me I wasn't the right person for the job, they would give me advice about what the right job would be. On one occasion, the hiring manager said, "You aren't a good fit here, but John over in the development program has a position opening soon, and it sounds like you'd be the perfect fit over there; let me give you his number so you can call him."

This had never happened to me. Instead of being a generic person who could do everything, which looked like every other person interviewing for the job, being honest allowed these managers to understand who I was and identify where I would fit in their organization. I found a job within a month, far earlier than almost all of my other classmates. The manager who hired me even said I wasn't the best fit for the position, but he expected another job to open soon where he would transfer me, and that's exactly what he did. The job fit me like a glove and I loved it.

Since then, I've worked in several different positions and companies and fit well in some, and not so well in others, and often the difference came down to what my manager valued.

Then, Fredi took a job in Washington state. While shutting down our home in Arizona, I found a modeling and simulation job at a space travel company near Seattle that fit my background and experience. Having always wanted to go to space, I was thrilled when they flew me out for an interview. When I walked into the lobby, the atmosphere felt awesome. The hallways were filled with science fiction memorabilia, easily recognizable from the movies, and a central common meeting area was dominated by a two-story, steampunk-styled fireplace that looked like a spaceship out of a Jules Verne novel. I was spellbound.

As a prospective employee, I was given a tour of the facility where I was invited to sit inside a real space capsule that was someday slated to take astronauts into space. As I walked along the factory floor, surrounded by computer-controlled machines two or three stories tall, I was awe-inspired by the incredible technology and development surrounding me. I could have spent a month learning how these machines worked and would have gladly done so for free.

The hiring manager told me the interviewing process would last most of the day. First, I would give a presentation to the team about my background and a difficult problem I solved, and then I'd go through several one-on-one interviews with each member of the modeling and simulation team.

After completing my presentation, which went quite well, I was invited to have lunch with the team. As we talked, it became clear I had something in common with each of them. From sky diving to scuba diving, from having children to sharing the company's vision of space, we talked non-stop through lunch. By the time we were done, I felt this group was more than just a bunch of potential co-workers; someday, we would become friends.

After lunch, the one-on-one interviews began. The first team member, a young man in his early twenties, met me in a common area and I watched as he sketched out a fuel pumping system on a blank piece of paper. He then began asking me questions. He was presenting me with a fluid dynamics problem, a topic I hadn't studied since school, and while I made some general comments about pressures and volumes and flows and such, I was unable to answer his questions. I hadn't prepared for this. He caught me off guard. However, I decided not to let it bother me; I had four more interviews to go.

I walked into the next interview, where I was met by a man closer to my age. On his blank piece of paper, he drew an airplane climbing into the sky and asked me about the various forces affecting its airframe. In engineering, this is known as a free-body diagram. I took the paper and drew in some arrows, but then began to reconsider. The plane's angle of attack into the wind wasn't quite right, so I began erasing and redrawing several of my lines and arrows until I thoroughly confused myself. I could tell he wanted me to succeed, the two of us had connected during lunch, but as hard as I tried, I wasn't able to recover.

Flustered, I walked into my next interview, where even the simplest questions confounded me. At one point, I couldn't even remember the units of pressure. I sat there thinking about it, *pounds per what is it again*? One after another, the questions continued to come, and by the end of the interviews, I'd morphed into a babbling idiot.

I thanked the hiring manager and suggested the job wasn't for me. I walked out of the building, fell into my car, and sat in the parking lot for over an hour. How could this have happened? I felt so confident during my presentation and all through lunch. I clicked with each member of the team. It was like I'd already earned the job, but then hit a wall.

I felt ashamed. I was embarrassed. I wasn't a rocket engineer; I was a fucking moron.

When I got home, I told Fredi what happened, and after listening and expressing her sympathy, she told me that the job *just wasn't meant to be.*

That wasn't helpful.

Just wasn't meant to be is an expression that people use on losers. They say it, to make you feel better. They say it, so you can blame the heavens instead of taking responsibility for your failure. They say it, so that you don't have to admit that you weren't smart enough, didn't try hard enough, or couldn't perform well enough.

I knew the truth. I didn't get the job, not because of some kind of cosmic intervention, but because I fucked up the interview. Or so, that's what I used to think.

Engineers are as diverse as their different personality types. Some are bean counters, making sure every digit of every calculation is precise and accurate to the highest degree, while others are movers and shakers who build systems with tremendous speed and skill. Some are human computers, who regurgitate equations and remember every formula they've ever seen, while others are more like me. I'm a bloodhound. I see patterns in data. I'm good at understanding and figuring out how different parts of a system work together. I'm adept at locating hard-to-find problems and bugs that elude other engineers. I dive deep into systems to understand how they are impacted by change. I'm more of an analyst than an engineer, and that's why I didn't get the job.

After sulking for a few days, I finally understood what Fredi meant when she said the job just *wasn't meant to be*. I sucked in that interview, not because I suck, but because I wasn't the right guy for the job. I'm terrible at recalling formulas, which is why my cubicle is always plastered with random equations and diagrams. I'm horrible at multi-tasking and answering quick and simple questions because my mind takes time to dive in and understand all the nuances of a system. Had they been hiring an analyst to look over the work done by other engineers, I might have been the right choice, but that's not who they were looking for. The job just wasn't meant to be, not because it was the will of the gods, but because I had applied for a job that wasn't right for me.

In the past, I've told others that it's not worth changing jobs because the grass isn't necessarily greener on the other side of the fence. Fredi has since proven me wrong. The grass might be greener, but you'll never know unless you take a look. And that's what Fredi did; she taught me to look. She taught me to look for the type of grass I want to sit in. She taught me to find a job that fits my strengths and a manager who shares my values. She taught me to be authentic, no so that they could interview me, but so I could interview the company to see if it was the right one for me.

I guess on the day of my interview, I just got distracted by all that cool shit. Maybe it was the steam-punk fireplace, or those huge machines, or maybe it was because I got to sit in a real-life space capsule. Whatever it was, the magic would have eventually worn off, and I would have ended up in a job that wasn't right for me.

In the end, I took a job with the US Space Force's Space Operations Command (SpOC), now known as Combat Forces Command (CFC). CFC is located in a modern building with bright skylights and an open atrium that houses some very cool models of satellites, but that's not where I ended up. My office was a few blocks away in an old building that was built many decades ago. In that building, the lights flickered in the hallways, the atrium was filled with moths that entered during the night, and the slow-moving elevator was known to trap unsuspecting visitors who hadn't been told it was safer to take the stairs. The bathroom fixtures were a dark beige, reminiscent of the 70s, and the stalls were so narrow that I had to sit angled on the seat to keep my knees from hitting the toilet paper dispenser. The office I sat in was warm, sometimes getting up to 90 degrees in the summer, but none of that mattered to me because...

I fucking loved that job!

24

THE MESSAGE

"OK, here's my plan. Let's purchase some land in the mountains, buy a camper to visit on the weekends, and once we retire, we can build a nice home."

"Why wait for retirement?" Fredi asked

"Because, by then we'll have saved enough money to afford a nice place."

"But if we both love the mountains, why wait till retirement?"

"Because our jobs are here in the city."

"Well, then let's find some new jobs!"

"I can't; there aren't any space-related jobs in the mountains."

"Then let's find a home in the mountains that is near a city with space jobs."

"I don't know... the commute might be too long."

"How about we rent a house in the mountains and find out?"

"Ok. I guess so..."

If I'd stuck with my plan, we'd still be living in the city and would've remained there for another 20 years. Instead, we rented a house in the mountains, spent a year or two looking at properties, and eventually purchased a tiny cabin infested with mice that just happened to be located on an awesome piece of property. After tearing out all the floors, drywall, electrical wiring, and plumbing, we remodeled it with the help of Fredi's stepdad and then moved into what has become, and probably always will be, our little mountain home.

Fredi knows what she wants and a comfortable environment ranks high on that list, which is why she constantly adapts her world to suit her. For instance, when she interviews for a job, she'll often ask, "Can I paint my office and bring in some lighting?" When the interviewers say, "Yes", I'm not sure they're aware of what she had in mind. Let's just say that when Fredi changes jobs, I know it's time to rent a moving truck. That's why when people visit her at work, they often say things like, "Wow, your office is more comfortable than my home!"

However, it's not only with her environment that she takes such care, but with herself as well. Fredi gets more compliments than anyone I know. Every time we go out in public, someone compliments her outfit, her jewelry, or the way she styles her hair. And for all those compliments, it doesn't seem she has to work that hard. She can be out the door in less than 30 minutes, and will likely be wearing something that came out of a thrift store.

I'm not sure how she does it; she just seems to have a natural eye for knowing what looks good. Well, that and a willingness to invest the time to find exactly what she wants. If Fredi wants to eat vegetables, then she has no qualms about spending a morning driving across town to a farmer's market or grabbing a shovel to dig herself a garden. She'll spend hours in the kitchen preparing just the right recipe and doesn't mind working an extra shift to pay for an expensive bottle of wine and the best cut of meat. When she decorates our house or her office, she'll spend weekends driving hundreds of miles to buy the perfect chair or piece of artwork.

Sometimes, when I'm helping her pick up a random piece of furniture, I get annoyed, because to me it seems like a waste of time. That's because I don't care what my chair looks like, nor what color my office is painted. I don't need to spend hours looking for just the right thing at yard sales because I don't mind wearing a shirt I picked up at a random store. And with prices these days, I certainly don't mind chewing on a cheaper cut of beef. That's because I'm practical.

I also happen to be thrifty. Fredi likes to get periodic massages and occasionally go to expensive restaurants. When I see some of these bills, I cringe. I tell her, "Honey, we need to save; we're still paying off our debts", but she doesn't listen; she just waves me off. Over time, I've given up trying to change her. I figured that she acts this way because she wants to create a calm and comfortable environment to counter her tumultuous and abusive upbringing. I concluded that since she was raised on food stamps, she decided that she'll never eat crappy food again.

But then, maybe I'm wrong...

Maybe she acts like this because she values herself enough to commit the time, effort, and money to treat herself right. Maybe she does this because, deep in her heart, she knows she's worth it. She knows she deserves to be surrounded by nice things, deserves to eat good food, and deserves an occasional massage to help her relax. Maybe she does all these things because her message to herself is that she's valuable, precious, and worthy enough to occasionally enjoy the finer things in life.

Which then got me thinking... what message have I been telling myself?

Meh, it doesn't matter... I live in the mountains! I mean, what the hell was I thinking, "Let's wait until we retire". Pffft, what an idiot!

I tell ya, without that woman, I have no idea where I'd be...

25

HAPPY ISN'T HARD

I f you asked me today whether I'm a happy man, I'd think about it and say, "Sure, sometimes I'm happy." I've come to understand that happiness isn't a state we can achieve and remain in, but an emotion we experience when we enjoy a special moment in time.

Before meeting Fredi, I was searching for a type of happiness that doesn't exist. I was operating under the belief that if I had the perfect wife, the perfect house, and the perfect job, then I'd be happy. But no matter how hard I tried, happiness always felt just out of reach.

Fredi calls this the *I'll-be-happy-when* syndrome. It's a false notion, one dependent on what I own, what I do, and who I'm with, and not on how I'm feeling inside. It's a belief often fostered by a parent like my dad, who wanted us to become doctors regardless of what we excelled at, judged our girlfriends irrespective of how we felt about them, and ridiculed any notion that didn't align with his own.

People talk about living in the moment, and while it always sounded like a good idea to me, I wasn't capable of doing it. I couldn't live in the moment because my mind was too cluttered with distractions. It was occupied by insecurities and feelings of unworthiness. It was bound up in the anger and resentment I incorrectly attributed to other people. It was distracted by my efforts to prove I was better than other people and in my futile attempts to gather false pride to generate self-esteem.

How can you live in the moment when all that stuff is happening in your head? I was so wrapped up in the fears of the past and was trying so hard to control my future, that I was unable to see the things that were happening right now, and right now is all we have. The past is over, and the future is uncertain, so all we can experience is now.

Paying attention to the present is probably the only reason I fell in love with Fredi. It wouldn't have happened otherwise because I wouldn't have given her the chance. I only dated her to distract me from my past by using her to fill the void left by my mistress. But from the start, Fredi challenged me to focus on the present. She did it when she sent me to the workshop and taught me to pay attention to what was going on inside. She did it each time she questioned my thoughts, my feelings, and the stories I made up in my head. There were times when I was ready to leave her, and as those fidgety and restless feelings took hold, I realized it was only happening because my mind was asking future questions; questions like, *is she the right person for me, will I find someone better down the road*, or *do I want to spend the rest of my life with her?*

I wasn't living in the moment, but worrying about the future, so I'd remind myself that the future is uncertain and that I didn't need to have all the answers. I'd tell myself that just because I was with her today, it didn't mean I had to be with her tomorrow. Those thoughts helped me uncouple the future and the past from the present and helped me calm down so I could ask better questions. Right now, questions. Questions like, *am I enjoying this moment with her, right now?* And when I asked myself those questions, the answer was usually yes, and the more times I asked, the more times I said yes, until one day I discovered... I'd fallen in love.

If happiness can only be found in the moment, then you've got to be paying attention to the moment to feel happy. When I was mired in all my shoulds, I couldn't live in the moment because there was always something about it that should have been different. My shoulds were creating so much drama and shit that I needed something really big and exciting to capture my attention. Something like the adrenaline dump of a SWAT mission, the excitement of an affair, or the thrill of receiving a blowjob at 30,000 feet. Those were the types of events that were needed to capture my attention, which is why happiness had been so difficult to find.

However, once Fredi helped me clear the crap out of my head, I found it didn't take as much to make me happy. These days, it takes only small things, like when I solve a complex problem at work, when the two of us spoon together in bed, or when we cook a meal together and eat it sitting side by side.

Fredi didn't help me find happiness, she helped me clear the stories from my head. She helped me find serenity, and once you have that, it's a lot easier to notice, appreciate, and enjoy the smaller things in life.

It becomes much easier to feel... happy.

PART V

STUFF YOU FIND AT THE END OF A BOOK

AFTERWORD

Ok, how do I say this?

Writing a book is fucking hard!

First of all, how do you tell a story like mine? I wasn't sure, so I read a bunch of blogs about memoirs and they all seemed to suggest I should write it like a novel, which would have been fantastic! I mean, what author doesn't want to write a great self-awareness story like *Wild*, by Cheryl Strayed, or *Eat, Pray, Love*, by Elizabeth Gilbert?

The problem is that those ladies are both experienced writers, and as much as I tried, I just couldn't come up with a clean storyline that encapsulated all of my insights. Making matters worse, I'm an engineer, and that's not a blessing when writing a book; it's a handicap. That's because I don't know how to skip past details that people intuitively understand, nor do I know how to generate tension or excitement using only my words. Instead, I want to add charts and graphs and have this burning desire to describe every association between every insight, which makes my narrative about as interesting to read as a service manual for a 1979 Toyota Corolla.

Clearly, writing a novel wasn't going to work for me. The best

I could do was write a few short stories, so I thought, maybe I could place each of my insights into their own chapter and use a short story from my life to illustrate a particular issue. I figured I could start each chapter from the perspective of how I saw the world before the insight occurred (so that guys like me would think, "Hey, that's how I see the world too.") before transitioning to how I see the world now (so that guys like me would think, "Whoa, that's a better way of seeing the world!)

Excited by this prospect, I came up with an outline and carefully ordered my chapters, starting with the simplest dysfunctional thought patterns first, before progressing into those more complicated ones that overlapped one another.

To keep the reader's attention focused on me and my dysfunctions, I decided to keep the other people in my story vague and simple, kind of like cardboard cut-outs that serve as stand-ins for me to interact with. That's why I didn't give most of the people in my book names, but used terms like ex-wife and mistress instead. The one exception I made was for Steve, the computer guy, who was such magnificent a character that he demanded a masculine name to offset his feminine appearance. Just for clarification, that wasn't his real name; I'm not even sure what his real name was.

Once I had all those details figured out, I began writing. I wrote during my weekends and I wrote through several vacations. I wrote when I should have been sleeping, and I wrote when stopped at traffic lights on my way to work. I wrote, and wrote, ands wrote, and then, I was done.

I had written 20,000 words, which is about 44 typed pages of single-spaced sentences on legal-sized paper. Now, to the non-writer, this may sound like a small number of pages, but when I accounted for the much smaller pages of a hand-held book, the larger font size, and the extra space between lines, my memoir suddenly grew to a whopping... 68 pages?

Crap!

Disappointed, I looked up word counts for books on the internet and discovered a typical memoir is about 60,000 words. So, I went back to writing. There were times when I blasted through chapters, and times when I wrote, erased, and rewrote the same sentence over and over again for most of the day. As I hacked out some of my favorite passages, the ones that ultimately failed to move the story forward, I learned what writers mean when they say that you must, "kill your darlings". I experienced many other things as well, like the frustration of not being able to find *just the right word* in a thesaurus, and the irritation of wanting a comma where the grammar checker insisted none should be. It was a challenging undertaking, but after four years, I experienced the joy of victory as I gained confidence my book was finally complete.

Eager for feedback, I sent my masterpiece to friends and family, and that's when I discovered the guys who were most like me, didn't like it. These were the guys I'd written my book for, but instead of telling me how it changed their lives, they called my insights obvious and said that they didn't think anyone else would be interested in reading it. The worst part is that I agreed.

Or at least, I thought that was the worst part.

The worst part was actually when Fredi told me that you can't write a story like this with the intent of helping other people because everyone experiences the world in their own way and therefore needs to follow their own path. I didn't have it in me to start over. I'd written everything except for the five chapters found in the section titled, A CLOSER LOOK, and I might have abandoned my efforts if it weren't for the single question that continued to elude me.

If my insights were so obvious after I discovered them, why hadn't I noticed them before?

I didn't understand how I could have managed to survive for

over forty years thinking I had been doing everything correctly without knowing how screwed up I'd been. While this question was still dancing around in my head, I read my chapter titled, THE APPLE THAT DIDN'T FALL FAR FROM THE CHRISTMAS TREE, to Fredi's family, and their tearful response and encouraging words led me to write the chapter called JUDGMENT DAY, which then gave me a glimmer of hope that someone might enjoy reading my book after all. I mean, if those emotionally disconnected guys didn't want to read my book, then maybe would their wives? Would my writing help them better understand their disconnected husbands?

Encouraged by this thought, I decided to press on. It took another year to discover and write the chapter titled, THE SAINT, which finally answered the question of why I couldn't see my dysfunctions. Unfortunately, answering that question raised another...

What had Fredi done to me, anyway?

While I knew I had come to love myself, by what means I'm still not sure, why did I suddenly feel connected to all those other people at the end of the chapter titled, ME BIG MAN, ME WEAR BIG CONDOM? While Fredi had given me some clues, such as, *before loving others you must first love yourself*, I didn't yet understand what that meant.

It would take another year of thought and spontaneous late-night revelations before I'd figure that one out, after which I wrote DEATH OF A SAINT, IN A WORLD OF MORONS, ASSHOLES, AND ME, and finally, SHITSTORMS CAUSED BY SHOULD.

Now, as I sit here writing these words, it has been six long years since I wrote my first chapter and I know that if I hold onto this book any longer I'll find more questions that need answering. So, I've decided that it's time to publish and see where the story takes me. I have chosen my title out of the hundred or so I've written, and have settled on the back cover narrative that I've iterated on since the very beginning. During this time I've read hundreds if not thousands of blogs about writing, attended writing events like the Pike's Peak Writer's Conference, and have spent hours learning about copyrights, ISBN's, and LCCN's. I've captured the name of my website, arranged for a professional photo of Fredi and me, and researched and purchased software with which to format and edit my book. I've spent hours learning about publishing options, thinking about keywords, and searching Reedsy.com to find the perfect cover designer (which I finally did!)

Next, I'll send my book out for some professional reviews, research marketing tips, build my website, and, finally, at long last...

publish my book.

And that's why writing a book is so difficult because, after all that writing, research, doubt, and endless decision-making, I still have no idea whether anyone will want to read it.

But if they do...

and you just happen to be one who did...

I have a request:

Please rate my book. Not only will your words help me market the book to those who enjoy it (and not to those who don't), but they will help me answer the one big question that still remains... was all of this effort worth it?

With that said, thank you so much for reading my story; I do hope you enjoyed it! Even better if it made you laugh or think! And if instead you have concluded I'm a jerk, which apparently some readers already have, that's OK too, because learning I was a jerk is what provided me the grace to be able to accept and love myself, which then led me to accept and love other people, and how beautiful is that?

I only wish more people could find their inner jerk, I think the world would become a better place.

With that said, may your life and the lives of your loved ones be filled with serenity, happiness, and a complete lack of should.

I wish you well,

Dan

ACKNOWLEDGMENTS

First and foremost, I would like to thank my wife, Fredi.

Without her, this book wouldn't exist... literally.

It's taken me six years to write it while working a full-time job, which means I wrote primarily during the weekends, holidays, and throughout several of our vacations. Her patience and understanding in allowing me this time, while helping me talk through my various issues, is more than I could have possibly asked for.

More importantly, I would like to thank her for putting up with 15 years of my bullshit and having the patience and dedication to help me become a better man. However twisted her judgment might be for spending this amount of time and energy on me, I am grateful that she has chosen to do so because there is no one I'd rather be with than her.

I'd also like to thank Dr. Paul Fitzgerald and his wife Susanna who are the founders of the Heart Connexion Breakthrough workshop. This is the workshop I attended with my brother in Kansas City, and over a period of 25 years was responsible for improving countless lives. While I dearly wanted to recommend this workshop to my readers, the Fitzgeralds have retired from this massive time commitment. I'm happy to say that Dr. Paul has opened up a small part-time private practice, and is now available at www.pauldfitzgerald.com. He just may be the most positive and energetic person I know.

While I have asked many people for feedback, I'd especially like to thank Donna McMurtry for her thoughtful notes, impressions of my writing, and pages of helpful hints that have served to significantly improve the flow and content of this book. Being an experienced writer herself (writing under the pseudonym D.D. Adair with her sister Diana Adair), her talents at spotting my novice mistakes were evident and greatly appreciated.

Also of particular note are Brett Collins, Francesco Zargani, and Michael Prochoda, who, after numerous iterations of this book, have inspired me with their honest feedback to keep digging deeper and further into my dysfunctions, thereby helping me, not only to understand myself better, but to ultimately drive me to expose the identity of the elusive saint. Thank you, gentlemen, for helping me add this most valuable layer to my book.

I would also like to thank Diana Adair, Fern Kishbaugh, Roy Adair, Tiffany Kishbaugh, Logan McMurtry, Deepak Gopalakrishnan, and Paul Deanello for reading and or allowing me to read various portions of this book. Allowing a writer to share their story is a fantastic gift, and I sincerely appreciate your time in letting me do so!

Thanks to all of you (and to those whom I surely neglected to mention), I appreciate the support you have given me!

www.ingramcontent.com/pod-product-compliance
Lightning Source LLC
Chambersburg PA
CBHW020233130626
46549CB00005B/1861